Happy Father

DAPDY!

I Love you!
June 19th, 2005

♡, Elizabeth

Your first
fathers day!

THE POCKET BOOK OF

Civil War
Weapons

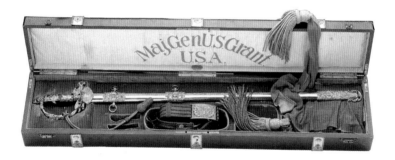

THE POCKET BOOK OF

Civil War
Weapons

ANGUS KONSTAM

CHARTWELL
BOOKS, INC.

This edition published in 2004 by
CHARTWELL BOOKS, INC.
A division of BOOK SALES, INC
114 Northfield Avenue,
Edison, New Jersey 08837

Produced by Salamander Books Limited
· The Chrysalis Building
Bramley Road, London W10 6SP

CREDITS
Editor: Shaun Barrington
Designer: Cara Hamilton
Reproduction: Anorax Imaging Ltd.
Production: Don Campaniello

ISBN: 0-7858-1919-3

Printed and bound in Malaysia

Page 1: General Ulysses S. Grant's silver and gilt sword was made by
Schuyler, Harley & Graham, New York.
Page 2: A great variety of handguns was carried by Union cavalryman;
and the variety was probably even greater for Confederate horsemen.
Page 3: One-hundred-pounder Parrott gun at an embrasure, Fort Brady
near Dutch Gap, Virginia, December 1864.
Page 5: A Park Ranger at Lookout Mountain, the Chickamauga and
Chattanooga National Military Park.

CONTENTS

INTRODUCTION

The American Civil War (1861065) has been described with good reason as the first modern war. The conflict has captured the popular imagination ever since for a variety of reasons, one of which stems from its position as a conflict set in a time of great technological change. It was also one of the first thoroughly documented wars in history. High literacy levels meant that many participants wrote an account of the part they played during those momentous years in American history. Large amounts of written records survive, cataloguing everything from the pay, medical and service records of individual soldiers to priceless documents such as the original copy of the Act of Succession, the Gettysburg Address, or the Appomatox articles of surrender. The publication of 127 volumes of *The Official Records of the War of the Rebellion* provides us with access to a level of

Below: *Thomas J. Jackson's forces struck the Orange and Alexandria Railroad on August 26, 1862, capturing the Union supply depot at Manassas Junction. John Pope's Army of Western Virginia was forced to retreat. Supply lines–as in all wars–would play a key part in this war, including railroad and river.*

Left: *Piles of ammunition lie amid the ruins of Richmond iron works in 1865. World War I is often referred to as "the first machine war." Such scenes challenge that assertion.*

information that was never available in earlier conflicts. Since then millions of words in print on the subject have covered virtually aspect of the war and the personalities who played a major part in it. The war was probably the first to be extensively photographed, so we have been left with a first-hand visual record of the events which took place, and a clear picture of how the soldiers dressed, lived and fought.

Another form of visual reminder of the conflict is found in a host of museums, battlefield interpretation centers and private collections, where original artifacts used by the soldiers still survive, from personal possessions, uniforms, and weapons to the remains of warships and fortifications. For the first time we can put a face to a name, touch a coat worn by a soldier, or walk the deadly space crossed by those soldiers almost 150 years before. For many it remains a personal event in the recent past; they identify directly with those who fought and died on those battlefields.

Below: *Union infantry uniforms and equipment. For the Federal troops, equipment was usually in good supply and of standard quality. The weapons are the Model 1840 non-commissioned officer's sword and Model 1842 rifled musket.*

Above all, the Civil War was fought at a time when the established way of life was changing. The spread of industrialization and the growth of cities, the revolution in transportation which resulted from the invention of the steam engine and the social evolution resulting from a growing influx of immigrants all had an impact on America during the mid-19th century. The country was no longer a rural landscape where settlers struggled against nature. The country was changing, and so too were the people. The Civil

War was not even confined to the States. Irish immigrants fresh off the boat were encouraged to join the Union ranks, while German settlers from Pennsylvania, Scots from North Carolina, and Frenchmen from Louisiana all answered the call to arms. While many of the weapons used in the conflict were produced in either the North or the South, significant quantities were imported from Britain, France, and European countries as diverse as the nationalities appearing on the docksides of New York or Boston.

Some of these influences come across in this study of the weapons used during the conflict. It highlights the difference between the industrial power of the Union and the Confederacy, and the degree to which both sides were prepared to improvise in order to acquire the weapons they needed. The ingenuity of the inventors and arms manufacturers supplying the Union were only matched by that of the Southern designers and machinists who struggled to produce guns and other weapons which could be the equal of those produced by their mass-producing, industrialized adversary. This was matched by the courage and skill displayed by the captains of Confederate blockade runners, who ran the Union blockade to bring the Confederacy the British-manufactured arms and equipment it needed to survive. Above all, a study of the weaponry used by the protagonists allows us to place ourselves in their shoes, and better understand what it was like to load a rifled musket under fire, or to ram home the charge in a field gun when the enemy were advancing toward you. Finally, the book traces the development of weapons during a revolution in military technology, and helps explain the impact these changes had on the men who had to stand in the firing line.

SMALL ARMS

Contrary to some accounts, despite the immense difficulties, the Confederates did not lack lag behind the North in personal firepower. Through home manufacture and imports by blockade-runners, they usually had a sufficient supply of small arms, most from abroad. Their rifles were equal to those used by the Union and fair breech-loading carbines were made in Richmond for the cavalry; though Union cavalry firepower was eventually superior.

Right: *The 48th New York Infantry at Fort Pulaski, 1862. Two million men would need equipping in the coming years. To put the logistical demand in perspective, there were more full generals during the War than there had been engineers of all ranks in the tiny pre-war US Army.*

The Infantry Musket

The outbreak of the Civil War coincided with a military revolution, where new technology was rendering existing weapons obsolete, and the effectiveness of infantry firepower was dramatically improved. Until a decade or so before, the standard infantryman's weapon was the flintlock musket, the same firearm used by the soldiers of George Washington. It had remained in use since its first inception in the late 17th century, and by 1700 the flintlock had become universally accepted as the weapon of the foot soldier. Over a century later the US Army still employed an improved version of the same musket, itself based on a French pattern first introduced in the mid-18th century.

The way the flintlock musket worked was relatively complicated compared to the simple mass-produced weapons that succeeded it. In almost all cases a cartridge was pre-made, consisting of a ball and a charge of powder, all rolled together into a paper container. When the soldier was ready to fire his musket he would grab one of the cartridges from a pouch, bite off the end of the paper tube,

Above: *The famous "Brown Bess" flintlock was the standard British Army infantry weapon throughout the Napoleonic Wars and was standard issue for English troops during the American Revolution. Despite the 300-year-old design, flintlocks like these would see action in the Civil War on both sides.*

Below: *1853 Pattern Enfield rifle, by far the most numerous imported firearm of the War.*

then pour a small portion of the loose powder into a small pan in his gunlock. An L-shaped device known as a frizzon would then be snapped in place over the pan, which kept the powder in place until the gun was ready. The soldier would then stand his gun on its butt, and pour the remainder of the loose powder down the barrel of his weapon, followed by the ball and the remains of the paper. He would then take a ramrod out of its holder on the underside of the gun barrel, and tamp the charge home until it rested at the back of the barrel. The gun was now ready to fire. When ordered he would point the gun at the enemy, then snap back the cock of his flintlock mechanism. This consisted of a piece of flint, clamped between two steel jaws. When the trigger was pulled the flint would snap forward, striking the L-shaped plate, forcing it backwards to expose the pan. At the same time a spark would be created, which would ignite the priming charge, which in turn would set off the main charge inside the barrel. Its greatest drawback was that the process was slow, and the musket was liable to be rendered ineffective in wet weather. While hunters and specialist infantrymen used rifled pieces, the majority of military flintlock longarms were smooth-bored. It was a tried, tested and effective infantry weapon, and used by every modern army in the world during the early 19th century.

The percussion cap changed all that. First developed by the Reverend Forsyth, a Scottish preacher in the 1820s, the percussion system relied on a percussion cap for its ignition system; a small copper cup filled with fulminate of mercury, which ignited if struck. A nipple was pierced by a vent, which ran into the base of the barrel, and the cap was fitted over the nipple. When the cap was struck by a hammer the resulting spark set off the main charge, just like a flintlock

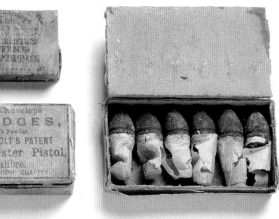

Left: *Union ammunition and accouterments. Clockwise from top left: percussion cap box; percussion caps; British-made Ely brand of caps for a Colt; pistol bullet mold; pistol tool; .44 paper cartridges open and (left) closed; .31 paper cartridges (above); Lawrence primers for the Sharps carbine (above center); various caliber metal and paper cartidges— the smallest being a .44 metal cartridge for the Henry repeating rifle and the largest a .58 caliber ball paper cartridge.*

piece would. What was different was that this type of gun could be fired in virtually all weathers, and was faster to operate.

To load and fire the weapon the soldier stepped back with his right foot, and dropped the butt of the musket to the

Right: *12th New York State Volunteers. Mustered in 1861, Their list of ensuing engagements can hardly be rivalled, including First and Second Bull Run, Seven Days' Battle, Antietam, Fredericksburg, Chancellorsville, Gettysburg, and Spotslyvania. It is unlikely—if he survived— that the soldier on the far right would have retained his side arm right through the War. Handguns were often sold, traded, or abandoned as useless burdens.*

ground near his rearmost foot. With the muzzle pointed up and away from him. Like the flintlock he took a self-contained cartridge from his cartridge box, with a measure of powder and the bullet wrapped together in paper. He would bite the end off and pour the powder down the barrel

Left: A reenactment of Pickett's Charge during the Battle of Gettysburg, one of the most dramatic episodes of the War. Across a front more than a mile wide, General George E. Pickett's division and a division under General James J. Pettigrew plus other brigades advanced across open ground toward Cemetery Ridge. The accuracy and takedown power of the infantryman's weapon by 1863, coupled with the range and lethality of artillery, made such a frontal assault against well-placed defenders on good ground an obsolete tactic. Nearly half of the attacking force of some 13,500 were killed, wounded, or taken prisoner. Some of those few who got as far as the Federal lines engaged in hand-to-hand combat, an extremely rare event throughout the whole of the War.

Above: *Confederate troops at the Warrington Navy Yard, Pensacola, Florida, in 1861. Much of the rebel camp equipment was civilian in origin pressed into service, as was the weaponry in the early stages of the War.*

shoving the paper and the bullet after it. He then removed his ramrod, turned it around and tamped the bullet down to the end of the breech with it. Sometime soldiers didn't replace their ramrod, but just stuck the metal rammer in the ground beside them, which speeded up the operation slightly. The soldier then brought his left hand to the balancing point of the musket, around its middle, and then held the gun outward at waist level, the gun's butt held against his thigh, the muzzle pointing at the enemy. He half-cocked the hammer and slipped off the old copper percussion cap, which he kept on during the loading process as it prevented air getting into the barrel, which could lead to a premature discharge when the powder was being poured into the barrel. He then pulled a new percussion cap out of a small pouch, and fitted it over the nipple. His musket was now loaded and ready to fire. When he wanted to fire the weapon he would pull the cock back all the way, put the musket butt to his shoulder, aim and pull the trigger. The procedure was a little simpler and quicker than that for firing a flintlock musket, and the weapons were usually a little shorter, meaning they were more manageable, and even more importantly, they could be fired in the rain. A well-drilled soldier of the Civil War could get off three shots per minute, although the average rate of two shots per minute was more common.

During the decades before the outbreak of the war the US Army had adopted the percussion system, and several variants of percussion-operated muskets had entered service. Another improvement was the introduction of reliable rifled weapons, which improved both range and accuracy. Previously, rifled guns had been slow to load, and

Below: *A Confederate regiment drilling near Mobile in 1861, no long arms in evidence. It is all too tempting to make a case for the inevitability of Northern victory because of the superiority in quality and quantity of its manufactured arms. This is however overly simplistic. The South was well armed, though certainly "outgunnned" in the last year of the War by Union artillery.*

were considered the preserve of specialist light infantry units, who were trained to make the best possible use of their weapons. Limited numbers of rifle-armed soldiers proved highly effective during the American Revolutionary War, and again during the War of 1812 against Great Britain. By the time of the Mexican-American War (1846-48), the accuracy of rifled guns had improved considerably, as had their popularity with the army. Pure rifles still had a use, but it was felt that the accuracy they imparted was so much greater than conventional smoothbore muskets that a system needed to be invented which would allow regular non-specialist soldiers to benefit from rifled weapons. Thanks to experiences gained during this conflict the US Government commissioned a study into equipping the bulk of its infantry with rifled muskets. Unlike pure rifles, these weapons were loaded like older smoothbore weapons, but when the bullet was fired the lead expanded, making contact with a series of rifled grooves on the inside of the barrel.

During the early 1850s most European armies had adopted their own version of this type of weapon, and during the Crimean War (1854-56) the superiority of the rifled musket over its smoothbore counterpart was demonstrated when British and French units consistently outshot their Russian opponents. American designers perfected their own version of the weapon, and the result was the Springfield rifled musket, the weapon of choice for the Civil War soldier. The key to its design was the projectile it employed. Known as the minié ball, it was named after its French designer, Captain Claude Etienne Minié, who had first developed the projectile for use by his own national army. The minié ball was a conical bullet with a hollow base which was smaller than the interior bore of the gun, allowing

Opposite: A *group of Coldstream Guards from the Crimean War carrying* Minié *Rifles. This rifle gave the British superiority in firepower over the Russian smooth-bored muskets. The* Minié *ball would be far and away the prime killer of the* Civil War.

it to slip down the barrel without jamming, even when it was wrapped in the remains of its paper cartridge. This paper cartridge contained both the powder and the minié ball, the paper serving as wadding, which would help contain the blast during the weapon's initial ignition.

Right: *Confederate infantry equipment. The weapons are the Fayetteville rifle and Model 1860 Colt Army revolver. The side knives almost certainly would not have been used in battle, but would have been indispensable tools in camp.*

When the powder charge went off the bullet's sides, or skirt, expanded, and the bullet gripped the rifling on the inside of the barrel. The rifling gave the weapon much great accuracy and the expanding bullet meant that speed of loading was not reduced. All in all it was the ideal weapon

Opposite: *2nd Rhode Island Infantry in camp. It is fascinating to look at rosters and orders of battle and speculate about what lies behind the bare facts given. Take David Hay of 2nd Rhode Island Volunteers, Company F: enlisted 6/6/61; deserted 11/13/61; returned 12/9/62; deserted 1/24/63. What personal drama was played out over those 18 months?*

Following pages: *The Henry rifle was a derivative of the Smith & Wesson/Volcanic Arms, with Henry's modified action and improved cartridge. The "rimfire" cartridge was a brass casing with the propellant in its base. 1 Early brass frame Henry. 2 and 3 Iron frame, 2 levered for loading. 4 engraved brass. 5 and 6 Early production brass frame, silver plated, with .44 caliber rimfire Henry cartridges. 7 Early military rifle and wooden cleaning rod. 8 to 11 Late production military Henrys with characteristic crescent butt.*

of the period. Its effectiveness was demonstrated during the Civil War. By the time the smoke cleared some 200,000 men had been killed on both sides during the conflict, and over 500,000 men had been wounded. It has been estimated that some 90% of these casualties were caused by the minié ball.

Equipping the Armies

Once the war began both sides had to equip the thousands of untrained volunteers who flocked to the colors. Just under 40,000 modern rifled muskets were available in North America, the majority of these weapons housed in US Armories or State Arsenals spread across the country. Most of those located in Southern States were seized by the Confederates, and the weapons used to arm their recruits, so that by the time the fighting started both sides had access to a limited number of modern weapons. The rest of the recruits were armed with whatever was available; smoothbore muskets, smoothbores converted into rifled muskets, and even flintlock muskets of the American Revolutionary era! As the war progressed both sides attempted to introduce some kind of standardization, but even the industrialized North was never able to fully equip all its infantry with the same type of weapon. This said, certain weapons, such as the Springfield Model 1855 percussion rifle musket, or the improved Model 1861 version of the same weapon were mass-produced by both sides. Over a million Model 1861 rifled muskets were produced during the war, and while the South could not hope to match Northern industrial output, they managed to produce substantial runs of weapons in their armories.

Union forces were equipped with weapons from a range of sources, and a high degree of standardization was achieved

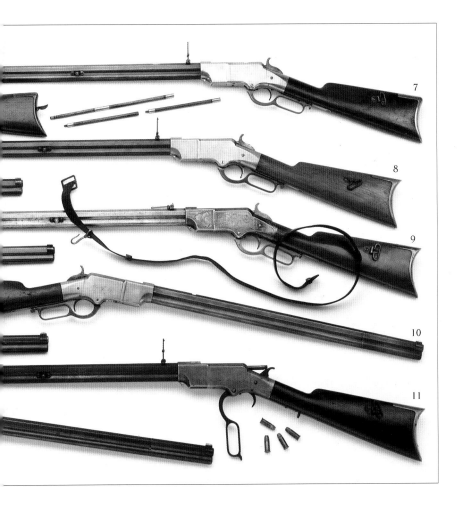

7

8

9

10

11

Below: *The relative sophistication of long arms would dictate effective range, from smoothbore, to rifled musket, to rifle and the very rare repeater.*

as the war progressed, although in most cases the issue of new weapons to troops in the Western Theater lagged behind the equipping of troops in the East.

Among the older weapons available at the start of the war was the Model 1842 (M1842) percussion smoothbore musket, of which 30,000 were available in State arsenals when the war began. Of these some 14,000 had already been converted into rifled muskets in Army workshops. The weapon began life as a flintlock piece, and had already been altered once, before the start of the Mexican-American War.

While less than ideal, it provided both sides with a useful stopgap while better weapons could be manufactured or procured.

A more useful weapon was the Model 1855 (M1855) percussion rifled musket, produced in the Springfield and Harper's Ferry Armories, and under contract by Eli Whitney, a private arms manufacturer. This was the first American gun to adopt the minié ball, but it was expensive to produce, and employed an alternative Maynard tape primer system which did not lend itself well to mass production, or to use by

Below: *These reenactors represent the heterogeneity of uniform and arms typical of many Confederate forces. Most have some kind of musket.*

largely untrained volunteers. For the most part this weapon was retained by the regiments of the old army, while volunteer regiments were equipped with converted smoothbores, or the less complex Model 1861 (M1861) percussion rifled musket. This became the standard small

Below: *Reeenactment of the Battle of Gettysburg. After the third day, both sides had lost a quarter of their army.*

arm of the war, with over 671,000 being produced in the North for use in the army, and tens of thousands more seeing service with the Confederacy, in the navy, or forming stockpiles in case of emergency. During the first years of the war the Union government balked at providing these expensive weapons to new volunteer regiments. After all, they were little more than poorly-trained militia. The Springfield weapons cost $13.95, compared to the $9 it cost to produce a smoothbore musket. Consequently large quantities of smoothbore weapons continued to be manufactured during 1861 and 1862, until public and military pressure forced the US government to switch to the production of rifled weapons.

It was soon found that the production of guns in both North and South was insufficient for the needs of the two armies, at least until the northern industrial centers could adapt themselves from the manufacture of commercial goods to the production of weaponry. As a consequence large numbers of guns were imported from Europe. The most popular imported design of the war was the British Model 1853 (P1853) rifled musket, known popularly as the Enfield after its British place of manufacture. In some ways it was a better design than the M1861 Springfield, so its issue was welcomed by both sides when they became available. This weapon and other British small arms accounted for three-quarters of all weaponry imported into the Union during the Civil War, and an even larger percentage of that smuggled through the blockade into Southern ports, to equip the Confederate army. Other foreign weapon imports included rifled muskets or even smoothbore pieces imported from Austria, Belgium, France and Germany. Of these, Austrian rifles were the most

Right: *This picture of troops under review at a regimental winter camp, Army of the Potomac, gives some indication of the sheer scale of the enterprise.*

Below: *Muskets and distinctive bearskins of militias in camp. There were several such uniforms on both sides at the beginning of the conflict. Such headwear would usually disappear when the real business of war began.*

commonly imported type, accounting for some 20% of the total number of imports. The remaining 5% was shared by Germany, Belgium and France, although the Germans maintained the largest share of the import market. Almost half a million weapons were imported from these four countries, as European governments and arms dealers grasped the opportunity to rid themselves of what they saw as obsolete firearms in their arsenals, or grasped the chance to increase the manufacture and export of their primary national firearm. In addition large quantities of rifled

muskets were produced in both Union and Confederate workshops, based directly on the patterns imported from Europe. Clearly the majority of these home-grown copies were versions of the Enfield rifled-musket, but other Austrian and German weapons were also copied by private manufacturers in the North.

The North also developed a significant technological advantage over the Confederacy, and were able to take advantage of a pre-war design for an experimental breech-

Above: *22nd New York State militia at Harper's Ferry, VA, 1862. During the Civil War, Harpers Ferry became one of many Union garrison towns where runaway slaves, or "contraband," sought refuge.*

Left: A *rare image of Confederate troops displaying uniformity. These are recruits being drilled at Fort McRee, Pensacola, Florida, in early* 1861. *In January* 1862, *Union artillery at Fort Pickens began an intense bombardment of rebel positions on the Pensacola-Warrington mainland and at Fort McRee. McRee was badly damaged. A few months later, the Confederates evacuated Pensacola, burning the fort.*

loader, the Model 1859 breech-loading rifle. As a result some 9,141 Model 1859 Sharps breech-loading rifles entered service in the Union army during the last year of the war, while similar carbines were even more widely issued to cavalry units. Another 12,471 Spencer repeating rifles were also acquired by the US Army during the conflict, along with 1,731 Henry repeating rifles. While the Sharps rifle used a linen cartridge, the Sharps and the Henry used brass ones, heralding a new form of durable ammunition which would become the standard type of ammunition after the war. However technologically superior these weapons were over the conventional percussion rifled muskets in service, their high cost made their widespread deployment prohibitively expensive, and in the end only a handful of elite sharpshooting units were issued with these revolutionary new weapons.

The Confederacy found itself at a distinct disadvantage in terms of the production of firearms, despite the seizure and removal to Richmond of the extensive facilities of the Harper's Ferry Arsenal, the largest government-run arms producing depot in the country after Springfield. It lacked any large arms-producing center of its own outside Richmond, but the Confederates managed to achieve a substantial output of weapons by improving the facilities they already had. Still, when the first Confederate armies took to the field whole units were armed with flintlock muskets or other old smoothbore weapons. During the war the Confederate army was equipped with firearms from these Southern depots, and from the importation of European firearms on board blockade running steamers.

However, their greatest source of weaponry and indeed all forms of military equipment was the Union army. A string of

Union defeats in the first years of the war produced a wealth of military booty. This continued on a lesser scale during the later years of the war; between the late summer of 1863 and the late summer of 1864, the Confederates managed to capture over 45,000 Union rifled muskets and other firearms, despite the fact that the tide of war was running against the Southerners. The majority of these captured weapons were Model 1861 Springfield and Pattern 1853 Enfield muskets.

Following pages: *Chaplain William Corby gives absolution to the Irish Brigade at the Battle of Gettysburg on July 2, 1863. Only 532 men remained of the Brigade and the losses were far from over; another 198 would fall there.*

During the first months of the war large quantities of US Army weapons were captured in Southern arsenals, meaning that both sides were able to field large quantities of the same types of weapon. What changed was that the Union Army could easily replace its battlefield losses, and replace obsolete weapons with more modern types. For their part the Confederates were reduced to a relative trickle of new weapons, and relied heavily on the capture of better-quality small arms from the enemy.

The result of all this was that an amazing variety of weapons saw active service. While attempts were made to standardize the variety of weapons within the same unit, this was rarely achieved until the full weight of Northern industrial production made itself felt after 1863. The weapons were issued as and when they became available, and were replaced as opportunity allowed. This meant that in many cases the same regiment could carry several different weapons, although this practice was more common in the Confederate Army than in the Union one.

The commanders of both sides tried to achieve some semblance of order out of this muddled supply of different weapons. The Confederate "Field Manual for the use of Officers on Ordnance duty" (1862) stated that the Confederate army was armed with a mixture of Springfield Model 1855 and Enfield Pattern 1853 rifled muskets, either originals or copied from them, Model 1840 and even Model 1822 smoothbore muskets (almost all of which had been converted into percussion weapons), plus the obsolete US Army 0.69-inch smoothbore musketoon, and 0.7-inch caliber imported rifles, usually from either Liege in Belgium or Brunswick in Germany. The M1822 smoothbore musket referred to in the manual was actually a weapon which

entered service as a flintlock in 1816 (becoming the M1816), and which remained in service in various forms until it evolved into the M1835 smoothbore musket. The Union Army also listed these same weapons in its arsenal, in addition to a host of imported rifled muskets. During the war or its immediate aftermath the US Government imported 226,294 Austrian, 57,477 Belgian, 59,918 German (more accurately Prussian), 14,250 French and 5,9995 Italian rifled muskets and other longarms in addition to the widely feted Enflield P1853 rifled musket. Most of these weapons were ones which had been rejected by the European powers.

An example of the mixed nature of small-arms supply is provided by the account of the Illinois Volunteer regiment. During a muster held in the last months of 1862 the regiment declared that it was equipped with 96 Springfield M1855 or M1861 rifled muskets, four Enfield P1853 guns, 143 Model 1842 smoothbore percussion guns which had been converted to rifled muskets, and 105 miscellaneous imported weapons; 72 Belgian 0.69-inch rifled muskets, plus 33 Austrian rifled muskets of various calibers, including 11 of the modern Lorenz rifles. In all these weapons used four

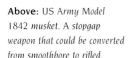

Above: US Army Model 1842 musket. A stopgap weapon that could be converted from smoothbore to rifled.

Below: US Army Model 1861 rifle-musket. This seems to have offered only marginal improvements over its three predecessors.

different sizes of ammunition, making the effective supply of the regiment something of a logistical nightmare. This mixture is typical of Confederate units throughout the war, and of Union troops during the first years of the conflict. In the Union army the tendency was that units in the Army of the Potomac or other Eastern Theater formations would be better equipped, and would achieve something akin to a standardization of weaponry, while those troops who fought in the Western Theater continued to be equipped with a range of weapons for much longer. Even this was something of a generalization, a Pennsylvania Volunteer unit which fought as part of the Army of the Potomac at Chancellorsville was still equipped with a mixture of Springfields, Enfields and foreign imports when the 1863 campaign began.

The Springfield Rifled Musket

Some of the basic types of weapon deserve to be described in a little more detail. The standard type of American-made percussion mechanism rifled musket of the war was the Springfield Model 1855, whether produced at Springfield, Massachusetts, or under contract by another Union supplier, or even when copied at the Richmond Arsenal in Virginia. Wherever it was produced, soldiers usually referred to it as the "Springfield". The piece had a 40-inch long barrel, a walnut stock, and measured 54 inches from muzzle to butt

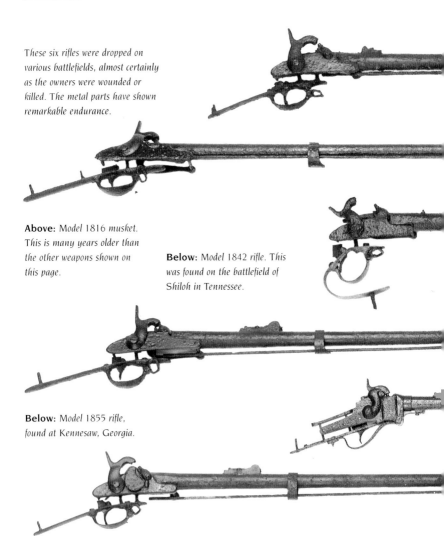

These six rifles were dropped on various battlefields, almost certainly as the owners were wounded or killed. The metal parts have shown remarkable endurance.

Above: *Model 1816 musket. This is many years older than the other weapons shown on this page.*

Below: *Model 1842 rifle. This was found on the battlefield of Shiloh in Tennessee.*

Below: *Model 1855 rifle, found at Kennesaw, Georgia.*

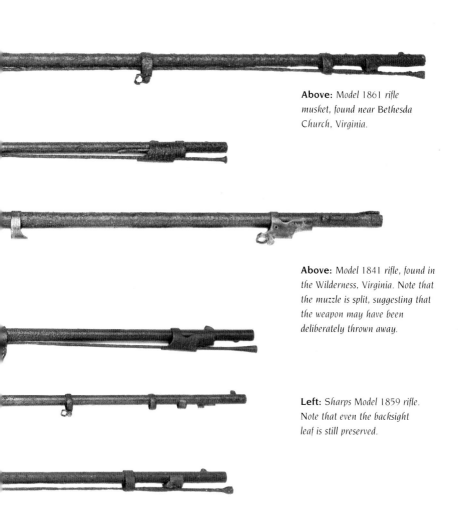

Above: Model 1861 rifle
musket, found near Bethesda
Church, Virginia.

Above: Model 1841 rifle, found in
the Wilderness, Virginia. Note that
the muzzle is split, suggesting that
the weapon may have been
deliberately thrown away.

Left: Sharps Model 1859 rifle.
Note that even the backsight
leaf is still preserved.

Right: *British Pattern* 1853
rifle-musket.

Below right: *Justice rifle-
musket, a* US Army *rifle-
musket from a private
contractor.*

plate. It weighed a little over 10 pounds, and was fitted with clips for a rifle sling, so the soldier could carry the piece on his shoulder. It had a caliber of 0.58-inch, and was a single shot, muzzle-loading weapon which fired the standard lead minié ball using the procedure outlined earlier. Previously, the US Army had used heavier 0.68-inch caliber musket balls for its smoothbore rifles, and 0.54-inch caliber conical projectiles for the rifles operated by Army sharpshooters. The introduction of the Springfield meant that the Army had begun the process of standardization on the 0.58-inch minié ball, similar to that used in most European armies of the time. An iron ramrod was carried in a housing under the barrel, and a wickedly-shaped 18-inch steel bayonet of a triangular section was designed to be clipped onto a special lug on the barrel, sited three inches behind the muzzle.

The Model 1855 (M 1855) rifle musket had an adjustable ladder-style sighting device fitted to the barrel a little forward of the end of the breech. It was graduated in 100-yard increments out to a range of 900 yards. When the gun

was first introduced it was designed to be used with the patented Maynard tape primer system, a device first invented by Doctor Edward Maynard, a New York dentist. The tap primer worked a little like a child's cap gun, with its roll of paper caps. A series of fulminate of mercury percussive charges were trapped between two thin paper tapes, and the whole strip was sealed and weatherproofed using varnish. When the gun was cocked a small arm pushed the paper strip forward, centering the next percussion charge directly over the firing nipple. According to Maynard the biggest advantage of his system was its cost; regular percussion caps cost the Army $1 per thousand, while Maynard's strips could be manufactured for a quarter of the price. The system was widely used in sporting guns and carbines, but it was simply too fragile for use as the ignition system of an infantryman's long arm. Problems with the feeding mechanism, and a marked propensity for the paper strips to become water damaged meant that the system was seen as unreliable. Maynard countered that it was less fiddly

Following pages:
Confederate and imported cavalry carbines and artillery musketoons. Several private contractors made these for the Confederate Ordnance Department. Cook and Brother made substantial numbers based on the English 1853 Enfield. 1 Dickson, Nelson, and Co. carbine. 2 J. P. Murray carbine. 3 British Pattern 1843 Enfield musketoon. 4 British Terry's Pattern 1860 carbine. 5 J. P. Murray musketoon. 6 British 1853 Enfield carbine. 7 Tallahasee carbine. 8 Tarpley carbine. 9 Le Mat carbine.

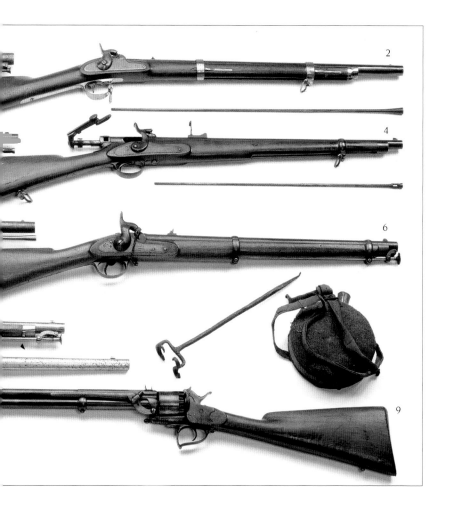

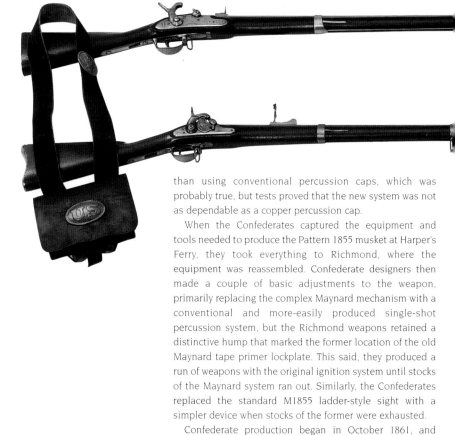

than using conventional percussion caps, which was probably true, but tests proved that the new system was not as dependable as a copper percussion cap.

When the Confederates captured the equipment and tools needed to produce the Pattern 1855 musket at Harper's Ferry, they took everything to Richmond, where the equipment was reassembled. Confederate designers then made a couple of basic adjustments to the weapon, primarily replacing the complex Maynard mechanism with a conventional and more-easily produced single-shot percussion system, but the Richmond weapons retained a distinctive hump that marked the former location of the old Maynard tape primer lockplate. This said, they produced a run of weapons with the original ignition system until stocks of the Maynard system ran out. Similarly, the Confederates replaced the standard M1855 ladder-style sight with a simpler device when stocks of the former were exhausted.

Confederate production began in October 1861, and would continue until the late summer of 1863. By that stage the Confederates found themselves with a surplus of captured weapons, so production was halted until the

Top: US Army Model 1816 *musket. A smoothbore weapon, shown here with its bayonet in place.*

Above: US Army Model *1855 rifle-musket, shown with rifle-musket cartridge box with shoulder belt. The successor to the Model 1842, the Model 1855 had a rifled barrel, which necessitated proper sights (note the raised backsight).*

surplus ran out. The war ended before production was resumed. When the war began the Model 1861 weapon was just entering service, but it would take several months for the Springfield armory to attain full production of the gun, or to sort out subcontracting deals with other manufacturers. Consequently the immediate wartime needs of the army were served by an increase in production of the M1855 musket, but with a slightly simplified (and cheaper) sighting device.

When the Springfield Model 1861 (M1861) rifled musket was introduced, it had abandoned the Maynard tape primer system, and had returned to a conventional percussion cap system instead. Otherwise it was essentially a shorter variant of the weapon which had preceded it. The other main difference between this Springfield musket and its predecessor was that it had a simple leaf-shaped site, graduated for ranges of 100, 300 and 500 yards.

Above all it was a cheaper weapon to produce, costing just $13 to make, or roughly half the cost of the M1855, and it was relatively straightforward to manufacture. This meant that when the war began, the North was able to begin the mass-production of these long arms, either in the Springfield armory, or in one of 22 private small-arms factories who had been subcontracted by the Springfield Armory. It became the most widely-used rifled musket of the war. Some 670,617 Springfield M1861 weapons were produced by the Union during the war, while the Confederates produced another 23,381 copies of the weapon in Richmond. The M1861 had an overall length of $55\frac{1}{2}$ inches, making it a fraction longer than its predecessor, although it weighed a little under eight pounds, or two pounds less than the M1855.

Left: *Burnside's winter campaign against the Confederate capital of Richmond involved the capture of the strategically important town of Fredericksburg. However, the events on the Rappahannock River would prove to be his undoing. The futile assault on Marye's Heights by no fewer than 14 successive Federal brigades would contribute to 12,000 Union losses.*

In 1863 the final variant of the M1855 was produced. One criticism of the M1861 was that its percussion hammer system had been modified to fit over the hump left by the Maynard primer, a result of saving money by not re-designing the lockplate. While not as distinctive as the hump on the Richmond-produced version, it was still a noticeable remnant of the older system. The Springfield Model 1863 replaced the hammer with a new, stronger version, and the lockplate was redesigned to remove all traces of the Maynard system. In the process the whole design was simplified, and an extraneous "clean-out" screw was removed from the gun.

The rifled musket gave the Civil War-era infantryman a reliable and effective weapon, with an accuracy which was far superior to smoothbore weapons. With a smoothbore musket it was considered unlikely that a firer could hit a target he was aiming at from 100 yards away. Its effectiveness came when large bodies of troops fired their weapons off in a concentrated volley, much as they had done on the battlefields of Europe during the Napoleonic Wars. The rifled musket raised the bar. At 100 yards a soldier firing a Springfield rifled musket could group his shots inside a four-inch wide bulls-eye on a target. The spread increased to nine inches in diameter at 200 yards, 11 inches at 300 yards, and 27 inches at 500 yards. This meant that at a relatively long range a bullet would consistently pass within two feet of the point the firer was aiming at. In theory both the M1855

and the M1861 could hit targets out to a range of 1,000 yards, but beyond 500 yards the accuracy dropped dramatically. Its true maximum effective range, where a soldier could be expected to hit a target he was aiming at, was considered to be between 500 and 600 yards. If the target wasn't a single man but a formation the size of a company of infantry; 100 men in a 16 yard-long line, then the chances of hitting something increased significantly. With a two foot deviation, a soldier might not hit the man he was aiming at, but he might well hit the soldier standing next to his target. This 500-600-yard effective range was fine on the testing range, but on the battlefield, with smoke, noise and confusion, the expected level of accuracy was far less. Most infantry commanders during the war expected troops armed with Springfield rifled muskets to be able to fire with great effectiveness at a range of between 200 and 300 yards. This had a profound effect on battlefield tactics. During the Napoleonic Wars, soldiers could maneuver in dense formations within 100 yards of the enemy firing line. During the Civil War any attempt to maneuver in this way was to invite prohibitively heavy casualties, forcing commanders to disperse their troops into more strung-out formations.

The Enfield Rifled Musket

The Enfield pattern 1853 (P1853) was widely regarded as being the best rifled musket of its day. Consequently it was imported in large quantities by both sides during the Civil

Above: *Impossible for anyone but an expert to know from this photograph, this is a reproduction of the Enfield Pattern 1853 rifle-musket, made in Italy. The market for such reproductions grew in the 1970s as reenactment societies flourished. The original weapon was also known as the three-band Enfield, for obvious reasons.*

Above: *A Confederate cavalry weapon, the British Enfield Pattern 1853 musketoon was a cut-back adaptation of the standard British rifle.*

War, and it was also copied and produced by American manufacturers working under license. In fact it was so widely imported that it became the *de facto* standard infantry weapon of the Confederate army, and second only to the Springfield M1861 in the Union arsenal.

The Union Army alone imported 428,000 of these guns, and the number used by the Confederates was also significant, and is estimated at 100,000. In addition to importing it, the Confederates also produced their own copies of the weapon, which were usually regarded as cruder, simplified versions of the original. The Southern workshop of Cook and Brother produced the best home-grown versions of the gun, but other locally produced variants proved less successful, and all were regarded as markedly inferior to the original.

The weapon was similar to the Springfield model 1855 musket, but it used a .577-inch caliber, the standard British bore size of the period. With an overall length of 55 inches and weighing 8.6 pounds it was comparable in size and weight to the M1861 and M1863 Springfields, but it could be easily distinguished because it used brass fittings for its nose cap, butt plate and trigger guard, compared to the steel fittings used on the Springfield weapons or their copies.

The gun had a barrel length of 39 inches, although a shorter variant also entered service during the war, a piece known to the British as the Pattern 1858 Short Sea Service Rifled musket, and to the Americans simply as the short Enfield. This shorter piece could be easily identified because it had two rather than three brass barrel rings linking the barrel and the stock together. (Many short Enfields were bought privately by British citizens who feared invasion by the French at this time).

Another feature of the Enfield was its distinctive sighting mechanism, graduated out to 1,000 yards, but in practice the weapon was only slightly more accurate than the Springfield, giving it an effective battlefield range of around 300 yards. Like the Springfield, it was designed to carry a simple triangular-section bayonet, and with a little modification the gun could be adapted to take both the Enfield and the Springfield bayonet designs.

Of the other European imports, the most common was the Austrian Model 1854 Lorenz Rifled Musket, a well-designed and reliable piece with a bore of 0.54-inch, but it was no better or worse than the Springfield Model 1861. Most of the 100,000 rifled muskets imported from Austria by the US Army were of this type, and a number fell into Confederate hands, or were brought into Southern ports aboard blockade-runners.

Above: *Model 1842 smoothbore musket amd socket bayonet.*

Smoothbore Muskets

By the time the Civil War began the smoothbore musket was considered obsolete. However, the large numbers of troops first went to war with these antiquated firearms because nothing better was available. When the war began the Confederates raided their State arsenals or captured US Army depots for firearms, and unearthed large quantities of these smoothbore muskets. Many weapons owned by individual states were flintlock pieces, of the kind used a century before. It was not until the end of 1862 that the Confederates managed to re-equip the bulk of their forces with rifled muskets. Of these, many were simply the older flintlock weapons which had been adapted to the percussion system in Southern workshops. These guns were then re-bored and rifled, so that they could fire the minié ball.

Among the weapons brought out of retirement were American copies of the British Short Land Pattern Musket of 1775 (better known as the "Brown Bess"), and the American Model 1795 and Model 1808 smoothbore muskets, both variations of a French design used by the armies of Napoleon. The Confederate "Field Manual" of 1862 mentioned earlier listed the Confederate arsenal as including .69-inch caliber Model 1822 and Model 1840 smoothbore flintlock muskets, so it clearly took some time for the Confederates to convert these old guns. These

weapons were actually a redesignated version of the Model 1816 and Model 1835 smoothbore muskets, the latter being an official percussion adaptation of the former weapon, a .60-inch caliber weapon which evolved into the Model 1840 (M1840). This was the last standard-issue flintlock musket adopted by the US Army, and some 56,000 were still held in

Below: *A mixture of muskets fire a volley at a reeenactment. The man in the dark blue shirt beneath the flag reaches for a percussion cap for his Enfield Model 1853.*

depots 20 years later, although by the time the war broke out almost half of these had already been converted into percussion weapons. In addition a similar number were stored in State arsenals. While the Confederates had little option but to press these obsolete weapons into service, the industrial capacity of the North meant that the Union Army was able to equip almost all its frontline troops with rifled muskets, keeping their smoothbore weapons back for use by second-line troops and State Militias.

Sharps New Model 1859 rifle.

Spencer breech-loading rifle.

Greene rifle.

Rifles

Both sides used purpose-built rifles in small numbers during the war. In most cases both the American and British long arms in widespread use during the war were also produced as rifles, the most common being the M1855 rifle. The only external difference between the Springfield Model 1855 rifled musket and the Model 1855 rifle was that the rifle had a shorter 33-inch barrel, secured to the stock by two bands rather than three.

There was no Model 1861 or Model 1863 rifle, although the Union Army imported some 8,034 Enfield Pattern 1858 Rifles, a short rifled variant of the P1853. Other commonly imported British rifles were the Kerr Rifle and the Whitworth Rifle (both 0.577-inch caliber weapons), while the 0.7-inch caliber Belgian and Brunswick Rifles were also used in limited numbers, particularly by the Confederates. The Confederates also produced their own rifle variants of the Springfield M1855 Rifle in a workshop in Fayetteville, North Carolina, the site of the North Carolina Armory.

Rifles were used by elite units of sharpshooters, and by men designated as snipers on account of their proficiency. It was expected that these men could use their rifle to hit a target with just a five-inch spread at a range of 600 yards, although the very best snipers were known to have been able to hit targets at ranges out to 1,200 yards. While it was harder and slower to load one of these rifled guns compared to a rifled musket, the accuracy of the shot was considered worth the loss in rate of fire.

Incidentally, most rifles were issued with sword bayonets rather than the usual plug bayonets used on rifled muskets. This was a tradition imported from Europe, where specialist rifle units wore their sword bayonet as a mark of distinction.

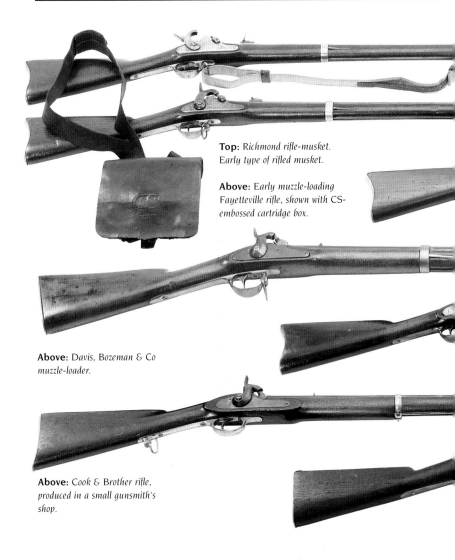

Top: *Richmond rifle-musket. Early type of rifled musket.*

Above: *Early muzzle-loading Fayetteville rifle, shown with CS-embossed cartridge box.*

Above: *Davis, Bozeman & Co muzzle-loader.*

Above: *Cook & Brother rifle, produced in a small gunsmith's shop.*

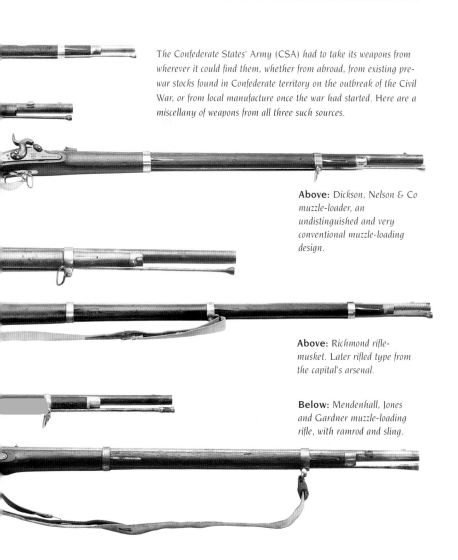

The Confederate States' Army (CSA) had to take its weapons from wherever it could find them, whether from abroad, from existing pre-war stocks found in Confederate territory on the outbreak of the Civil War, or from local manufacture once the war had started. Here are a miscellany of weapons from all three such sources.

Above: Dickson, Nelson & Co muzzle-loader, an undistinguished and very conventional muzzle-loading design.

Above: Richmond rifle-musket. Later rifled type from the capital's arsenal.

Below: Mendenhall, Jones and Gardner muzzle-loading rifle, with ramrod and sling.

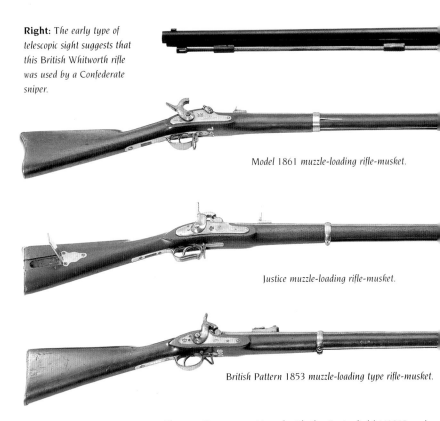

Right: *The early type of telescopic sight suggests that this British Whitworth rifle was used by a Confederate sniper.*

Model 1861 muzzle-loading rifle-musket.

Justice muzzle-loading rifle-musket.

British Pattern 1853 muzzle-loading type rifle-musket.

The practice was continued with the Springfield M1855 and the Enfield M1858 rifles, but during the war the Confederates adapted their own Fayetteville M1855 variants to fit a conventional bayonet. Although these guns were relatively unsophisticated compared with the elegant long-

barrelled hunting rifles in common use, they were perfectly accurate for the job they had to do. As the war progressed more sophisticated variants began to appear. For example the Henry 0.44-inch rimfire rifle designed by B. Tyler Henry was a lightweight weapon with a 15-shot tubular magazine housed underneath its barrel.

Some 13,000 of these weapons entered service with the Union Army during the war, and their all-enclosed metallic cartridges proved markedly superior to the paper cartridges used by more conventional firearms.

Another gun of note was the British-designed Whitworth rifle, a 0.451-inch caliber weapon which had been rejected by the British Army on the grounds that it was prone to fouling, making them difficult to use after only a few shots. However, of the 8,000 weapons designed by Joseph Whitworth, almost all were purchased by either the Union or Confederate governments. After all, a good sniper didn't require to fire his gun repeatedly, but would make every shot count.

Repeaters

Repeating rifles were used in limited numbers by the Union cavalry arm during the Civil War, although small quantities

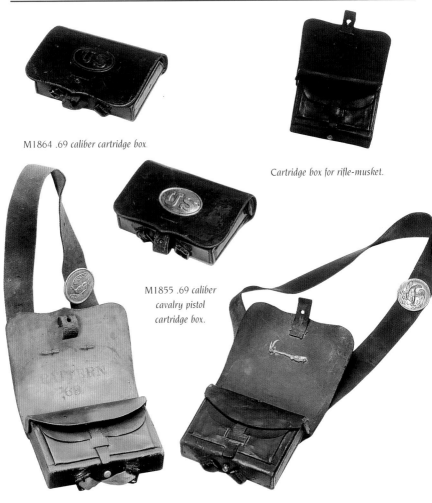

M1864 .69 caliber cartridge box.

Cartridge box for rifle-musket.

M1855 .69 caliber
cavalry pistol
cartridge box.

M1839 .69 caliber cartridge box.

M1855 .58 caliber rifle-musket cartridge box.

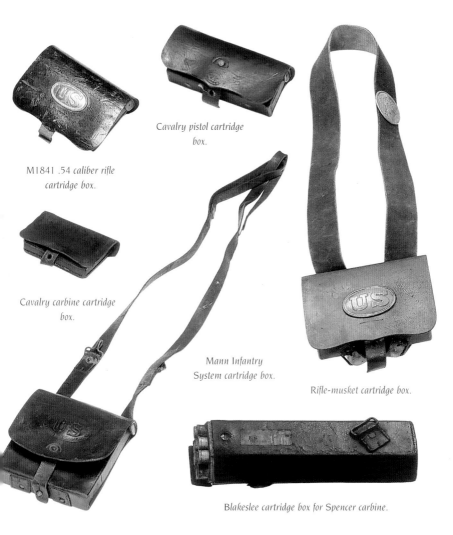

M1841 .54 caliber rifle
cartridge box.

Cavalry pistol cartridge
box.

Cavalry carbine cartridge
box.

Mann Infantry
System cartridge box.

Rifle-musket cartridge box.

Blakeslee cartridge box for Spencer carbine.

of these superb weapons fell into Confederate hands, although in these cases the specialist ammunition required for the pieces limited their value.

The technology which produced them was new, and many commanders and government officials viewed these revolutionary weapons with suspicion. They were considerably more expensive than single-shot weapons, they were time-consuming to produce, and it was generally felt that resources could be better spent producing a larger number of conventional weapons. Some commanders even thought that quick-firing repeating rifles would simply encourage troops to waste ammunition. The troops who used them had no such reservations, and were full of praise for their weapons. Two repeating rifles entered service during a war, albeit in relatively limited numbers; the Spencer and the Henry.

The Spencer had a short 30-inch barrel, and was a compact, elegant weapon. Seven 0.56-inch caliber brass

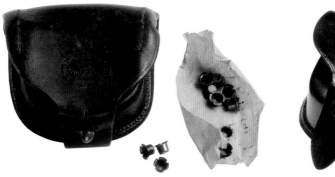

Percussion cap box with percussion caps as issued.

Circa 1863-1864 Union cap box.

cartridges were loaded into a spring-loaded tube which was inserted into the butt of the weapon. Every time the hammer was cocked and the trigger guard advanced the old cartridge was ejected and a new round moved up into the firing position.

The key was the round; a case containing the lead bullet and a 48-grain powder charge, encased in a single casing. It was fired when the hammer fell against the back rim of the casing, igniting the fulminate of mercury charge and firing the bullet down the rifled barrel of the gun.

This rimfire system was much more efficient that the normal percussion system, and would become the ignition system of the future. Guns of this type were used extensively in the American West during the second half of the 19th century, but the conservative nature of purchasers and senior officers meant that just 12,471 of these repeating rifles were purchased by the Army during the Civil War.

The Henry Rifle was a more advanced weapon, the brainchild of B. Tyler Henry. However, just 1,731 of these superb weapons were purchased by the army during the war. Unlike the Spencer its tubular magazine, which was housed underneath the 24-inch barrel, could hold no fewer than 15 rounds, giving the weapon a phenomenal rate of fire compared to other contemporary weapons. It fired a 0.44-inch caliber ball using a self-contained brass cartridge, similar to that used in the Spencer, and identical to that produced for the earlier experimental Volcanic repeaters. (See pages 28-29 for a selection of Henry rifles).

The Henry made up for its lack of sales to the Army by selling its guns to individuals, usually soldiers or officers who were eager to arm themselves with the best weapon

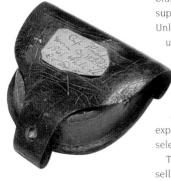

Circa 1861 *Union cap box.*

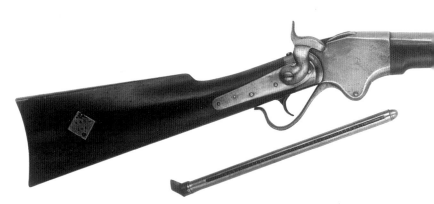

Above: *Once Christopher Spencer had demonstrated his repeating rifle to President Lincoln in 1863, a complete division of 12,000 men were equipped with it in the following year. Below is the tubular magazine holding seven copper rimfire cartridges, usually housed in the butt.*

available when they went to war—not a bad idea, so long as you could afford it. This meant that the total wartime production of the Henry rifle, including Army and civilian sales, actually totalled around 10,000.

They were mainly used by cavalry, and in battle troopers demonstrated the effectiveness of both the Henry and the Spencer during the final years of the war. One Confederate soldier claimed the Henry was: "that tarnation Yankee rifle they load on Sunday and shoot all week", a simple testimony to the effectiveness of the repeating rifle during the war.

Cavalry Carbines

The carbines was the weapon of choice for the cavalryman during the Civil War. Troopers needed a compact weapon which was shorter than a standard infantry rifled musket, so it didn't get in the way of the rider while he was on horseback, but it also had to be powerful enough to be effective when the trooper is mounted. For the most part cavalry fought on foot, using their horses to ride to and from the battlefield. In the rare occasions when they fought from the saddle, the carbine could be used as effectively as a shotgun or a pair of pistols. In almost all cases after the first flush of war, troopers on both sides preferred to rely on firearms than edged weapons in combat. They were simply more versatile, and more effective.

Most Civil War carbines had an overall length of around 38 inches, which compares favorably against the 55$\frac{1}{2}$-inch Springfield M1861 rifled musket used by the infantry. For the most part these weapons were single-shot percussion guns, although breech-loading weapons and even repeaters did see service. The Confederate cavalry tended to use single-shot weapons, as they were easy to produce in the small Southern gun workshops where they were made, while breech-loaders and repeaters were almost exclusively used by Union cavalrymen during the latter years of the war. However, the bulk of the Union horsemen still used single-shot carbines just like their Confederate opponents.

Of all long arms used during the war, carbines displayed the greatest variety of weapon types. It has been estimated

Above: *Joslyn Model* 1864 *carbine.*

that over 30 different types of carbine saw service during the war, a situation which was encouraged by the Union Army's policy of awarding production contracts to numerous small private weapon manufacturers.

For the most part these guns used cartridges similar to those used by the infantry, but wrapped in linen rather than paper. The idea was that the linen wrapping of the cartridge would burn itself off when the charge was ignited, leaving no residue in the barrel.

Unlike the infantryman, it was expected that a cavalry trooper would have to fire from horseback, meaning it was impossible to perform complex barrel-cleaning evolutions between shots. The carbine cartridges reflected this philosophy; the only reason why the superior linen wrap was not extended into use by the infantry was largely a matter of cost rather than efficiency.

Above: Smith carbine "broken" to permit reloading.

Above: Merrill late model carbine with breech open for reloading.

Right: Report for the Ordnance Office Construction Division on the Johnson's carbine, "with Rowe's improvement," March 1864. Rowe's improvement was supposed to ameliorate "the difficulty encountered in extracting the case of the cartridge after firing." In comparison with the Sharps carbine for this test, Mr Johnson's design was found wanting once again.

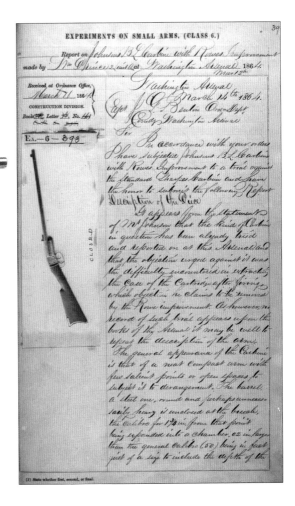

The most common carbine of the war was the Sharps M1859 breech-loader, the first mass-produced carbine to be acquired by the US Army just before the outbreak of the war. Other subcontracted companies such as Starr or Gwynn & Campbell supplied the Army with minor variants of the original Sharps design, but for all practical purposes the weapons were identical. Some 80,000 Sharps carbines were produced during the war, while Starr produced a further 25,000 and Gwynn & Campbell a little over 9,300 carbines of the Sharps pattern. These breech-loading weapons were easily operated either on the ground or from the saddle, and they were accurate.

The Sharps fired a 0.52-inch caliber bullet, a similar round to the Sharps rifle. The carbine was 39 inches long, allowing it to be fired using one hand if required. Even more importantly, it could be loaded and fired from the prone position, making it an ideal weapon for a skirmishing cavalryman. It was really a defensive weapon. While the cavalry manuals still required troopers to fight with swords from horseback, in practice cavalry commanders discovered that their men were much better used in a dismounted skirmish line, where they could rely on their carbines to hold off the enemy.

The Sharps carbine was sighted to 800 yards, while the Spencer carbine was expected to maintain its accuracy out

Opposite: *Federal column on North Market Street, Fredericksburg. The role of the cavalry was changing fast, primarily from an offensive "strike" force to a skirmishing, holding force.*

Below: *Spencer carbine with breech mechanism partly exposed and back sight raised.*

Above: *Sharps New Model 1859 breech-loading carbine, with back sight in raised position.*

to 1,000 yards, but it was soon discovered that these ranges were wildly optimistic. It was found that the effective carbine range regardless of the type of carbine being used was around 400 to 500 yards, while the most effective range was established at around 150 to 200 yards.

The way the Sharps carbine worked was fairly straightforward. By pulling on the levered trigger guard the breech block would be dropped, allowing the cavalryman to insert a linen-wrapped cartridge into the breech. By raising the trigger guard the breech would be raised back into place, and a small knife blade sliced off the rear of the cartridge in the same action, which exposed the powder inside to the flash from the percussion cap. The gun could then be fired, and the process repeated.

The Confederates lacked the industrial machinery needed to mass-produce breech-loading carbines, so they relied on cruder, home-produced versions of the Sharps carbine, known as the Richmond Sharps, or more commonly, they used captured Union weapons. The Richmond gun was never very successful, and only 5,200 were ever produced. The Sharps itself was plagued by gas leakage, and the seal on the weapon was never considered wholly satisfactory until the Model 1863 Sharps carbine entered service. The problem was finally rectified when the Model 1865 entered service during the last month of the war. The other difference between the M1859 and later models was that the new guns had iron rather than brass barrel bands, trigger guards and butt plates. By contrast the Richmond Sharps was even more prone to gas leakage than the original Model 1859 weapon.

Other Southern-produced breech-loading carbines such as the 0.52-inch caliber Tarpley carbine, or the Maynard, Morse or Perry carbines (which were all variants of the original Sharps design) were also produced in small quantities. However, there were never enough of these weapons to have an impact on the way Confederate cavalrymen were equipped in the field. This meant that for the most part Confederate troopers had to rely on single-shot muzzle-loading carbines such as the cut-down version

Below: *The Starr carbine was the fourth most popular rifle used by the Union soldiers. It borrowed many features from the Sharps, Smith, and the Burnside rifles, but its greatest virtue was its low misfire rate.*

Bottom: *Morse carbine. Another very early breech-loader, this example has its breech open for reloading.*

Right: Christian Sharps even succeeded in selling several thousand of his breech-loading rifle to the British Army for use by cavalry regiments in India. Left, from top to bottom: 1850 Sharps rifle with Maynard's tape primer; model 1849 with circular disk automatic capping system; Model 1852 0.5in-caliber carbine; rifle version with set triggers for hunting and target shooting; postwar model 1869 rifle. Right, top to bottom: Sharps rifle with repaired stock—some rifles were prone to breakage here because of recoil; 1874 Sharps (and below)—by then the legendary Winchester had arrived; earlier Sharps with adjustable sights on the stock; rare round-barrelled Sharps; and New Model 1863 rifle with 0.40 caliber shells.

Following pages: Union attack at Vicksburg. While Grant managed to drive Lieutenant General John C. Pemberton's men from the field outside the city, he could only take the city itself by siege.

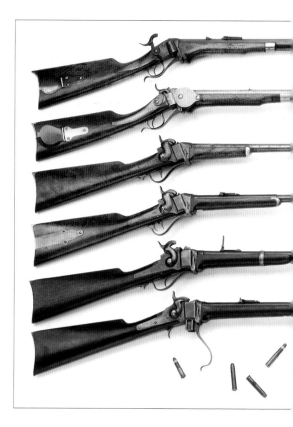

of the Springfield M1855 rifled musket. Some 2,800 carbines of this type saw service during the war, the conversion work being conducted in the Richmond Armory. The Confederates also relied on European imports, brought into the country

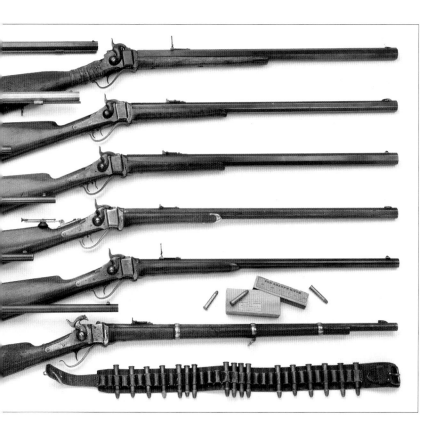

on board blockade-runners. The most common of these was
the British Pattern 1856 carbine, known to the British as the
"East India Pattern" carbine, and to the Confederates as the
Enfield carbine. By 1863 this weapon had become the most

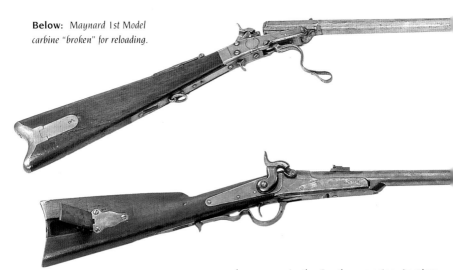

Below: *Maynard 1st Model carbine "broken" for reloading.*

common cavalry weapon in the Southern armies. Another feature of the Sharps carbine was its accuracy. In the hands of a first-class marksman, it could be used to hit a target the size of a man at 700 yards. This was comparable to a well-handled rifled musket, but what set the Sharps apart was its rate of fire, which was approximately three times that of a rifled musket, or six to eight shots a minute. This gave the dismounted cavalry trooper a significant firepower advantage over his opponent. When this was coupled with the ability to fire the carbine from a prone position, thereby reducing the risk to the firer, then the carbine was placed into a class of its own.

In addition to the Sharps, the US government also purchased some 94,000 Spencer carbines during the war, the shorter version of the Spencer rifle. These weapons first

entered service in 1863 and soon proved themselves to be extremely effective. Like the Henry repeating rifle they were popular with the troops who managed to acquire them.

Although they were a little longer and heavier than the Sharps carbine, they gave the trooper an unmatched volume of firepower, estimated at around 21 shots per minute; three times the rate of fire of the Sharps, and nine times that of a rifled musket. This was the next generation of cavalry firearms. The Spencer used a 0.52-inch caliber brass rimfire cartridge, and like the breech-loading rifles by the same manufacturer they were loaded into a long strip held in the stock. A fully loaded carbine could carry seven rounds in its spring-fed magazine, plus there was room for an eighth round in the breech. The trigger guard was pushed forward to cock the gun, ejecting the spent cartridge and sliding a new round into the breech. While it took a long time to load the long tubular magazines, the US Army surmounted this problem by issuing troopers with cartridge boxes containing several pre-loaded tubes. Reloading was a simple matter of unlocking the empty magazine, sliding it out then replacing it with a fresh one. While some troopers used Henry and Spencer rifles, the majority of carbines issued to Union cavalry units during the last year of the war were Spencer carbines. The Confederates simply had no answer to the firepower of late-war Union cavalry formations.

Above: *Joslyn Model* 1864 *carbine.*

Below: *Burnside 4th Model carbine, with breech mechanism partly exposed.*

Above: *Allen and Thurber Pepperbox pistol, made in Worcester, Massachusetts in the 1840s. The six barrels are bored out of a single block of steel. Until the advent of the percussion revolver these were the most popular repeating arms in the US.*

Handguns

There was more variety in the types and makes of handguns in the Civil War than in any other form of weapon. Soldiers of both sides carried a mixture of privately-bought guns, issued weapons, or whatever they were able to plunder from the enemy.

These ranged from the most modern revolvers to completely obsolete flintlock pistols, of the type carried by George Washington's cavalry almost a century before. Many were conventional single-barrelled guns, although some more bizarre handguns had multiple barrels, such as the novel Sharps four-barrelled 0.32-inch caliber rimfire pistol, or the more common 6-barrelled Pepperbox revolvers which were made famous by Mississippi riverboat gamblers. In the Union Army, supplies were usually available in large numbers, meaning that some degree of uniformity was achieved. However the Confederates had to rely on the import of weapons from overseas, and the home-grown production of handguns in improvised workshops, many of which were inferior versions of the original weapons. As was the case with other weapon types, Southern troops had to use what was available, or else plunder better-quality weapons from the enemy. Some types of guns proved extremely popular with the troops who used them, while others were soon rejected as being either too cumbersome or too unreliable. Many officers or even ordinary soldiers resorted to the purchase of their own handguns, in order to avoid having to use a greatly inferior issued weapon, or they took their own weapons with them when they rode off to join the army. For the most part handguns were issued only to officers, cavalrymen, and naval personnel in both the Union and Confederate armies, although other services were known to carry these weapons on occasion.

Below: *Virginia Manufactory Flintlock 1st and (bottom) 2nd model pistols. It seems astonishing that such weapons were still being produced at the outbreak of the War.*

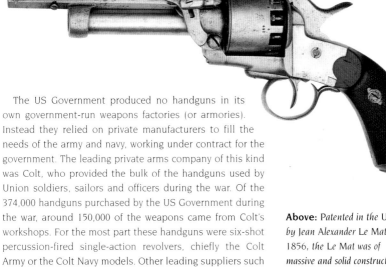

The US Government produced no handguns in its own government-run weapons factories (or armories). Instead they relied on private manufacturers to fill the needs of the army and navy, working under contract for the government. The leading private arms company of this kind was Colt, who provided the bulk of the handguns used by Union soldiers, sailors and officers during the war. Of the 374,000 handguns purchased by the US Government during the war, around 150,000 of the weapons came from Colt's workshops. For the most part these handguns were six-shot percussion-fired single-action revolvers, chiefly the Colt Army or the Colt Navy models. Other leading suppliers such as Starr and Savage produced their own handguns, or produced Colt weapons under license. The US Government bought just over 55,000 revolvers from the Starr Company during the war; 23,000 of their Starr Army Model 1859 single-action six-shot weapon, and then 31,000 of the improved 1862 Model, as well as 1,402 Starr Navy Model 1860 revolvers. The Remington company supplied the army with a further 12,000 copies of its Remington Army revolver during the war. Other even smaller manufacturers managed to sell their weapons to the army, who bought 5,000 revolvers from Rogers & Spencer, 1,000 from Joslyn, and smaller quantities from Allen and Wheellock and Pettengil, who had hitherto specialized in small civilian pieces.

Above: *Patented in the US by Jean Alexander Le Mat in 1856, the Le Mat was of massive and solid construction. The frame, including the butt, was made in one piece. A cylinder which held nine .40 caliber rounds fired through the upper barrel. The lower .63 caliber barrel held a charge of buckshot.*

Opposite: *Major General James Ewell Brown Stuart led Lee's cavalry with daring and intelligence. He was known to favor the Le Mat revolver.*

Above: *Lefaucheux pinfire revolver (top) and pinfire naval revolver (below). The pinfire cartridge had been invented in 1828, but really came to the world's attention at the 1851 Great Exhibition in London. The standing breech is fitted with a top-hinged loading gate with a spring catch. The round-barrelled version was selected by the French Navy in 1856.*

The US Navy bought 14,000 Whitney Navy revolvers, and 1,901 Remington Navy revolvers, both of which proved to be popular and reliable weapons. They also bought 11,284 Navy revolvers from the Savage Company, but these cumbersome weapons proved unpopular, largely because the mechanism used two triggers, one to revolve the cylinder and the other to fire the gun. By early 1862 the Navy had refused to buy any more, and the guns in service were soon withdrawn, and replaced for the most part with the highly reliable Colt Navy revolvers.

The US Government also bought handguns from Europe. Some 40,000 handguns were bought from British manufacturers, mainly the Adams Company but also from Deane, Kerr, and Chandler, all of whom supplied the British Army and the Royal Navy with weapons. Another significant supplier was the French company of Lefaucheaux, who supplied the US Army with 12,400 handguns.

Above: *Imported from Europe by the Confederates. From top: Beaumont-Adams; Kerr; Tranter with single trigger; Webley; and Tranter with double trigger.*

Above: *Colt Model 1849 pocket revolver, one of the many examples of Colt equipment used by the Union and captured by the Confederates.*

Right: *The Colt Model 1849 held by this corporal was almost certainly a studio prop.*

Samuel Colt's firearms company, based in Hartford, Connecticut, was the single most successful handgun manufacturer of the war. In the years before the war Colt's firearms developed a hard-won reputation for reliability and ruggedness, and it was inevitable that the company would become the leading supplier of handguns to the US Government when the war began. In addition to the sale of guns to the Government, Colt also sold weapons to individual soldiers who wanted a reliable sidearm, making him the single largest supplier of arms on either side during the conflict.

Several types of Colt revolvers saw service during the war. The Model 1851 Colt Navy revolver was a relatively lightweight 0.36-inch caliber weapon, with a single-action mechanism, which meant that the firer had to cock the piece by hand before each shot. The six-shot cylinder rotated into position each time the hammer was pulled back. Like almost all firearms of this period it had to be loaded by hand, with each self-consuming linen or paper cartridge tapped home into one of the six cylinders using the built-in rammer mechanism. Then, six percussion caps were fitted to each of the six nipples on the rear face of the cylinder before the piece was ready to fire. This was a time-consuming process, which meant that in effect, like almost all other revolvers, the weapon had a limited amount of firepower on the

Right: Brigadier General Jefferson Columbus Davis was one soldier we definitely know used a handgun in anger during the war, but we are not sure which model. While he was commanding a battalion under General William "Bull" Nelson during the organization of the defense of Louisville in 1862, the two argued in the bar of the Galt House in the city. Davis left and a few minutes later returned to shoot his commanding officer dead. Briefly incarcerated, he never stood trial and served with distinction for the rest of the war—but without another star.

battlefield. Although called the Navy, the revolver was also issued in limited numbers to Union cavalrymen, and the weapon proved the most popular privately-purchased firearm of the war.

The Model 1860 Colt Army revolver was a slightly larger 0.44-inch revolver which was renowned for its hitting power, and was the single most common handgun of the war, 129,730 copies of the weapon being purchased by the US Army between 1861 and 1865. Finally another Colt Navy revolver, the Model 1861 entered service with the US Navy during the conflict. A total of 17,110 Colt Navy revolvers of both types were purchased.

Top: *Colt Model 1848 Army.*

Above: *Colt Model 1860 with non-fluted cylinder.*

Right: British Adams Patent
revolver; its handsome
presentation box contains tools
and tins of percussion caps.

The cylinder, frame, and barrel of these revolvers were
made from hardened steel, while the trigger guard was
brass, and the grips carved from walnut. Interestingly the
bullets fired by these guns were larger than the diameter of
the base of each chamber, a method of ensuring that the end
of the powder charge fitted as close and as snugly to the end
of the firing nipple as possible.

Most of the handguns produced in the Confederacy were
crude copies of northern designs, but some home-grown
products were of better quality, although the number of
weapons produced was a fraction of those emerging from
the arms manufacturing companies of the North. The
Columbus Firearms Manufacturing Company produced

reliable weapons, albeit in limited quantities, but the most celebrated confederate revolver of the war was probably the Le Mat. This was an imaginative if not wholly practical design, invented by a Doctor LeMat, a Frenchman who settled in New Orleans before the outbreak of the war. His revolver was actually produced in manufacturing centers in France and Belgium, the Europeans working under contract for the Confederate government. The weapons were then

Above: *Confederate weaponry from small gunsmiths: Griswold and Gurnison revolver (top); and J. H. Dance and Brothers revolver (Below).*

Above: *Wesson and Leavitt dragoon pistol, .40 caliber; 800 were made, c.1850-1851.*

Right: *Remington-Beals Navy revolver.*

Above: *Remington New Model Navy revolver.*

Opposite: *George Maddox, a noted rebel guerilla fighter with Quantrill's Raiders, sports a pair of Remington New Model 1863 Army pistols. The chambers of the left-hand pistol are clearly loaded. Despite his dandified appearance, Maddox was a cold-blooded killer, both during and after the War.*

shipped to the Confederacy by blockade-runners after being shipped from France directly to the blockade-running ports of Nassau in the Bahamas and St. Johns in Bermuda. The revolver was manufactured in two different calibers, 0.35-inch and 0.4-inch, but in both cases a nine-shot revolving cylinder formed the base of the gun. The unusual feature of the piece, apart from its nine-shot capacity, was that this cylinder spun around another larger barrel, which was loaded with a single charge of buckshot, which fired out of its own smoothbore barrel sited beneath the main rifled barrel. In effect the Le Mat was a combination revolver and sawn-off shotun. It was only issued in limited numbers, but despite its awkwardness and weight it proved a popular sidearm, if for no other reason than it could deliver the greatest volume of fire of any handgun of the period! It is also remembered as being the weapon of choice of the Confederate cavalry commander J.E.B. Stuart. (See page 89).

The most common type of revolver issued to Confederate cavalrymen or sailors remained the Colt, either picked up on the battlefield or copied by a Southern workshop.

Below: *Union cavalryman poses with his Savage revolver. To cock the Savage, the middle finger was used to draw back the lever and then push it forward, cocking the hammer and rotating the cylinder.*

These Southern Colts were usually 0.36-inch caliber weapons, based on the Model 1851 Colt Navy revolver after the Confederate Ordnance Department decreed that this weapon would be designated as the standard Confederate sidearm. Some 14,000 saw service, but a lack of vital supplies and a shortage of suitable manufacturing facilities meant that the Confederacy could never hope at any stage to match the firearms manufacturing output of the North.

The largest Southern manufacturer of Colt copies was the Columbus Fire Arms Manufacturing Company mentioned above, whose 7,500 weapons were regarded as being as good as the originals, although the production method involved a simplification of the process used in the more developed Hartford mass-production workshop.

Griswold & Gunnison made 3,600 Colt copies, Rigdon & Ansley produced another 2,330, and other smaller manufacturers also contributed what they could, albeit it in relatively insignificant quantities. The company of Schneider & Gassick only managed to deliver 14 guns to the Confederate authorities, making it the smallest firearms manufacturer of the war!

One common design feature of Confederate versions of the Colt revolvers, apart from the caliber, was

that they were usually manufactured using brass rather than hardened steel frames, owing to the lack of suitable steel in the Confederacy.

In addition to replicas of the Colts, the Confederates also produced small quantities of other Union revolvers, most notably the 0.36-inch caliber Whitney single-shot piece, which was produced with brass fittings by the Macon Arsenal in Georgia and by the private firearms company of Siller & Burr. In all some 1,400 of these guns were produced by these two manufacturers during the war.

Above: *Starr Model* 1863 *Army revolver, .44 caliber.*

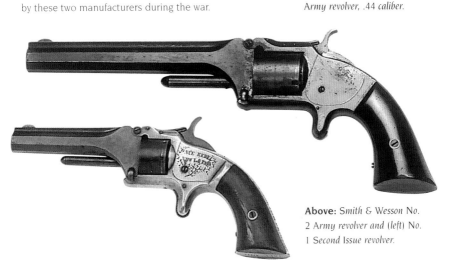

Above: *Smith & Wesson No. 2 Army revolver and (left) No. 1 Second Issue revolver.*

The Confederacy also imported handguns in large quantities, the weapons brought into the country on board blockade runners. The majority of these imported weapons came from Britain although French guns were also acquired. Like the Union, the Confederacy favored the guns produced by the Adams Company, while the 0.44-inch caliber Deane-Adams five-shot revolver was also popular, as was the Tranter, the Beaumont-Adams and the Kerr revolver designs. Like the Union, the Confederacy also bought guns from the French firm of Lefauchaux, but it also purchased from anyone else who it could do business with. As a consequence small quantities of French Raphael, and Perrin, revolvers and the Belgian-produced Houllier

Powder flask for recharging individual chambers of a revolver.

Pistol bullet mold device.

Powder flask.

Tools for use with rifle-muskets.

Tool for Colt Model 1860 Army.

weapons entered the South during the war, and even larger quantities of the highly reliable Blanchard revolver were also purchased in France by Confederate agents, then shipped to America. Of these French and Belgian imports the 0.45-inch caliber Lefaucheaux revolver was the most popular. Unlike other contemporary designs it used a pinfire method of ignition rather than percussion caps, and its ammunition was produced in brass cartridges.

It has been estimated that around 28,000 British and French revolvers were imported into the Confederacy during the war, which meant that imported weapons were more commonly found in Confederate units than home-produced weapons. However, the greatest source of firearms of all kinds for the Confederates during the war remained the US Army, whose battlefield losses outnumbered the total production and import quantities available to the Confederacy by conventional methods of acquisition or production.

Left: *Non-regulation holster for a Colt revolver (left); and a Remington revolver holster.*

EDGED WEAPONS

❖

While modern artillery and rifled small arms decided the outcome of battle, the old ways of war still played a part in the Civil War. Cavalrymen and most officers and NCOs on both sides were issued with swords, while almost all infantry carried bayonets to use in hand-to-hand combat. Although swords were more decorative or symbolic than practical, they were still widely carried, and were often used in combat. A case could be made for the humble knife being the most important edged "weapon;" at least it was useful in camp.

Right: *Union officers with regular-issue swords. Edged weapons were primarily a badge of rank by the mid-19th century.*

When the war began most volunteers imagined that cavalry would prove a decisive arm, and the newspapers expounded the notion of sweeping, decisive cavalry charges, where victory was won at the point of the sword. The reality of modern warfare in the mid-19th century

Right: The "Gray Ghost," Colonel John Singleton Mosby, the audacious and successful Confederate raider, with what looks like a standard cavalry saber. Such was the frustration the Union felt following Mosby's partisan raids, George Custer executed six of Mosby's men in 1864, and Mosby retaliated with seven of Custer's. A note attached to one of the bodies stated that Mosby would treat all further captives as prisoners-of-war unless Custer committed some new atrocity. The killings ceased.

Left: *Another dashing Confederate cavalryman, Brigadier General Turner Ashby, Jackson's trusted friend. At Harrisonburg, covering Jackson's rear, his horse was shot under him. He led his men on foot brandishing his saber: "Charge men, for God's sake charge." A bullet killed him almost instantly. Said Jackson on hearing the news: "I never knew his superior. His daring was proverbial."*

Following pages:
Confederate cavalry officers' uniforms and equipment. On the left is the sword of Lt. Gen. Wade Hampton. Despite his total lack of military experience or training before the war, Hampton turned out to be a superb military leader. Bottom center: saber made by Boyle, Gamble and Macfee. Right: saber of Major Heros von Borke, a member of J. E. B. Stuart's staff.

meant that this was completely unrealistic. The firepower of Civil War-era artillery and rifled muskets meant that cavalry were extremely vulnerable on the battlefield. They were also expensive to raise and maintain, so inevitably numbers were limited, at least until the closing year of the war when the Union was able to field whole corps of cavalry. This

vulnerability altered cavalry tactics. While the Napoleonic method was to use cavalry offensively, hammering their way through the enemy line, the firepower of the Civil War meant that cavalry came to be used defensively. Cavalry charges still occurred, and to some extent cavalry swords were still used, but primarily cavalry had become little more than mounted infantry. They would use their mobility to ride forward and seize a key piece of ground, then the troopers would dismount to hold it. Even in the few instances where cavalry fought against other mounted cavalry, the troopers of both sides tended to rely on their pistols and carbines

Opposite: *Not the most beautiful, but hopefully sound and with a stayer's blood. The horse was the cavalryman's most important equipment.*

Below: *1st US Cavalry at Brandy Station VA. Here 19,000 cavalry fought the greatest mounted battle ever in the western hemisphere.*

Below: *General George G. Meade's uniform blouse, hat and cap, sword belt and sash, field glasses, epaulets, presentation sword and two ornate scabbards.*

rather than on their swords. This meant that as the war progressed, the cavalry sword became relegated to the status of a secondary weapon, a symbolic object which denoted the status of the owner as a cavalryman, rather than a weapon which would be used in combat. In this respect it became similar to the infantry officer's sword, which was wielded more as a badge of rank and as a symbol of

Left: *Pattern 1851 Union cavalry officer's embroidered hat insignia.*

authority than as a weapon in its own right. A far more effective weapon was the bayonet.

The bayonet was first designed during the late 17th century as a means of giving infantrymen armed with muskets a chance of holding off enemy cavalry. Before the invention of the bayonet, a portion of every infantry regiment was issued with pikes, and their principal job was to keep enemy cavalry at bay. The introduction of the bayonet meant that these soldiers could be armed with muskets, increasing the firepower of the formation, while retaining its ability to protect itself against horsemen. During the 18th century the bayonet began to be used offensively, and in the hands of the British and Hessians during the American Revolutionary War it proved to be a weapon of battle-winning potential. A bayonet charge by professional European soldiers was often enough to make whole brigades of American militia flee the battlefield, and it was only when Congress raised its own regular troops armed with smoothbore musket and bayonet that the Americans had a chance of standing up to the British.

Above: Union Model 1840 *Cavalry saber.*

By the time of the American Civil War the use of the bayonet as a means of fending off cavalry was considered a thing of the past. Firepower was a much better guarantor of victory against enemy horsemen, while the bayonet was retained as a vital tool in hand-to-hand combat. During the battles for defensive positions such as the Sunken Road at Antietam or the Mule Shoe at Spotsylvania, both sides used the bayonet in melée. While it made the musket unwieldy it also provided the soldier with an important weapon during close-quarters fighting.

The Cavalry Sword

The typical cavalryman's weapon of the period was the saber, an elegant sword with a stout grip and a slightly curved blade. Traditionally European heavy cavalry carried straight-edged swords and light cavalry used sabers, but by the mid-

Below: Union Model 1840 *cavalry officer's saber.*

19th century the use of heavy shock cavalry was virtually a thing of the past, although units of this kind were still retained in most European armies. In 1860 the US Government issued its troops with a new light cavalry saber, which replaced the older Model 1840 heavy cavalry saber (or dragoon saber) whixch saw service during the Mexican-American War. However, stocks of the older sword were still retained by the army, which meant that both types of saber remained in service throughout the war. Also, both weapons

Right: *The "beau sabreur." As punishments go, sitting on the wooden horse to general derision for a few hours was not the most onerous.*

continued to be produced under contract by Northern arms manufacturers throughout the conflict, during which the US Army purchased 203,285 light cavalry sabers, and 189,114 heavy cavalry sabers for its troopers. In addition the army also acquired 1,279 cavalry officers' sabers, which were virtually identical to the model 1860 light saber, except they were more highly decorated, with additional engraving on the hilt and on the blade of the weapon.

Both the Model 1840 and the Model 1860 sabers were based on the French Model 1822 Light Cavalry saber, a weapon introduced into the French army following the experiences gained during the Napoleonic wars. Like the original model, the American sabers had brass hilts, the guard consisting of three protective bars topped with a swept-back pommel which was traditionally based on the design of a Phrygian helmet. This decorative feature was widely used in cavalry sabers around the world, and first appeared during the French Revolution as a symbol of liberty. The grip of the sword was constructed from wood, wrapped in leather then banded using strips of copper wire, giving it a metallic appearance. It was well-designed, and troopers reported that the grip was secure enough to allow the sword to be wielded with great effectiveness.

The Model 1840 heavy cavalry saber had a slightly curved hardened steel blade 37$\frac{1}{2}$ inches long, while the Model 1860 light cavalry saber was a little shorter with a 35-inch blade, but its curve was slightly more pronounced. The blade of the light cavalry saber was also a little narrower, measuring 1 inch across compared to the 1$\frac{1}{2}$ inch blade of the heavier, older model. Both swords were carried in metal scabbards, which tended to rattle when the cavalryman was on the move. Efforts were made to clad the inside of scabbards with

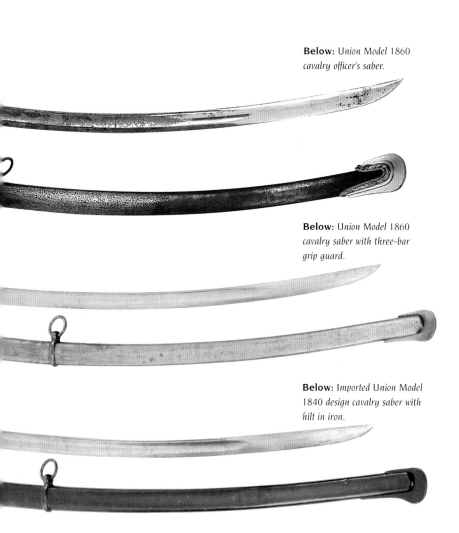

Below: *Union Model* 1860 *cavalry officer's saber.*

Below: *Union Model* 1860 *cavalry saber with three-bar grip guard.*

Below: *Imported Union Model* 1840 *design cavalry saber with hilt in iron.*

Above: *Ohio cavalrymen with their regular issue sabers with three-bar grip guards.*

wooden sleeves to prevent this, but these attempts were never wholly successful, and never received official sanction.

The Confederates also produced their own cavalry sabers during the war, direct copies of the Model 1860 light cavalry saber. In most cases these were cruder, less detailed versions of the original weapon, using oilcloth rather than leather around the grip, and using a simpler, untwisted strand of copper wire to bind the grip, which provided slightly less of a secure grip than the original twisted wire version. Another feature of Confederate versions of the saber was that the brasswork was generally redder in color than on Union sabers, owing to the greater amount of copper used in the production of brass for Confederate swords. Unlike the all-iron scabbards of Union swords, most Confederate cavalry sabers were housed in scabbards with brass mouths (chapes), while many scabbards were constructed wholly from brass. Being a softer metal, this proved more prone to damage than the all-steel scabbards used by Union troopers, and wherever possible the

Left: *Confederate Model 1840 cavalry saber in metal scabbard.*

Left: *Unmarked Confederate cavalry saber with scabbard made of sheet copper.*

Right: *Company 1 of the 6th Pennsylvania Cavalry, known as "Rush's Lancers," reputedly photographed in May 1863. The members of this unit were the cream of Philadelphia society. Many had served previously in the militia originally formed as George Washington's personal bodyguard, the First Troop Philadelphia City Cavalry. Perhaps it was this background that resulted in their taking into battle such absurdly outdated weapons as the lances on the left. They would soon be abandoned in favor of the carbine.*

Following pages: *Union cavalry artifacts. The saddle is a US Army model 1859 McLellan saddle. The rifle is the much-coveted Spencer repeating carbine. The lance was used by "Rush's Lancers" between 1861 and 1863.*

Confederate troopers replaced their own swords and scabbards with Union versions from the battlefield.

Sabers were not the only forms of edged weapons carried by cavalry during the war. When the conflict began several unusual formations were raised by both sides. One such unit

was the 6th Pennsylvania Cavalry, commanded by Colonel Richard Rush, which was raised from volunteers in 1861. While the troopers carried the usual cavalry weapons of light cavalry sabers and pistols, each man was also issued with a lance. These weapons were direct decendants of the cavalry

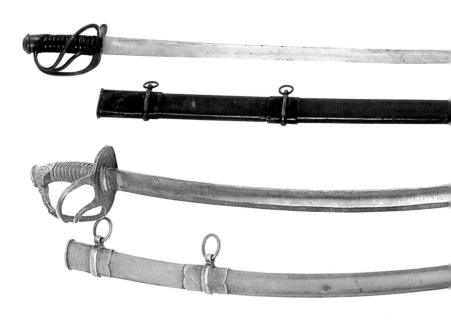

Top: *Unmarked Confederate cavalry saber with a wooden scabbard.*

Above: *Confederate cavalry officer's saber made by Thomas Griswold and Co.*

lances used by medieval knights, and while the weapon had fallen from favor during the late 16th century, it was revived during the Napoleonic Wars. Several lancer regiments were formed in the French Army during the early 19th century, and in the decades which followed lancer units were added to the strengths of several European armies. During the Crimean War of 1854-56 the British 17th and 21st Lancers participated in the foolhardy but romantic Charge of the Light Brigade during the Battle of Balaclava (1854).

Like a handful of his contemporaries Colonel Rush decided that the lance had a viable place on the American battlefield, so he issued his troopers with nine-foot long

lances made from Norwegian fir, and tipped with a triangular iron spike. Rush's Lancers used the weapon in combat during 1862, but in the following year the formation abandoned its quixotic medieval weapon and rode into battle with the more versatile carbine instead. A handful of other lancer units were also raised on both sides during the first months of the war, but these were soon converted into regular cavalry formations.

Non-cavalry Swords

Union officers and non-commissioned officers in all branches of the army and navy were authorized to carry swords of one type or another. These were largely designed to be decorative rather than functional, although on numerous occasions officers advanced into battle with their swords drawn, where the weapon served to encourage the men following on behind their leader. Needless to say this also made the officer more conspicuous, which was useful when leading troops forward, but it also served to attract the attentions of enemy marksmen. The Model 1850 Foot Officers' Sword was carried by company level officers; captains and lieutenants. This was a weapon with a slightly curved 32-inch steel blade, its surface heavily engraved. It had a brass hilt and the grip was wrapped in fishskin, then bound with twisted brass wire.

Below: *Confederate saber in the style of Nashville Plow Works, Tennessee, featuring a distinctive grip guard.*

Officers of the rank of major or above including general

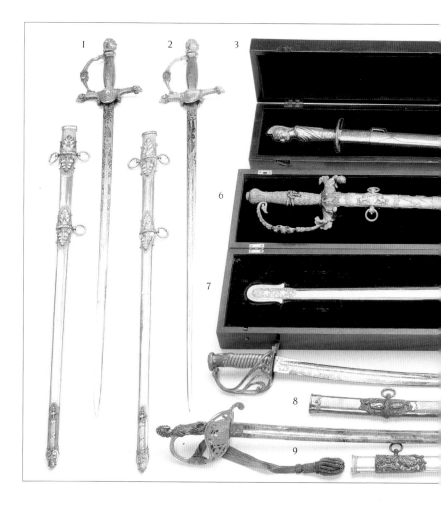

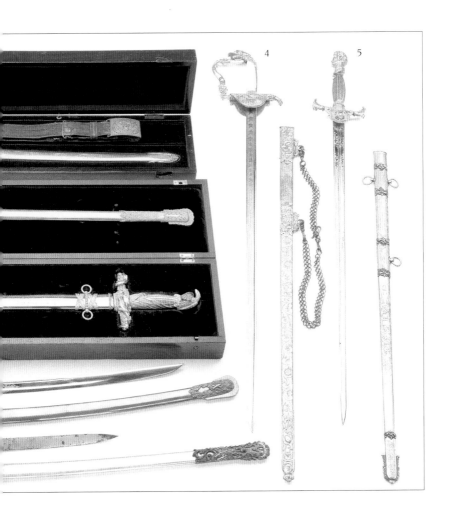

Previous pages: *Union officer's presentation swords. 1 and 2 Swords made by Tiffany, New York, and presented to Brigadier General Godfrey Weitzel, commander of the division occupying the right wing of the lines at Port Hudson; and Major General John M. Schofield, from 1888-95 Commanding General of the US Army. 3 Given to Brigadier General John Cook for gallantry at the capture of Fort Donelson, 1862. 4 Eaglehead sword owned by Colonel Sylvanus Thayer, Superintendent of the US Military Academy 1817-1833 whose reforms produced such commanders as Lee, Grant, Sherman, and Jackson. 5 Field officer's sword presented to Thayer by West Point graduates of 1820. 6 Presented to Brigadier General Charles Ferguson Smith. 7 Cavalry saber made by Ciauburg, Soligen, Germany, given to Major I. Townsend Daniel. 8 Sauerbier, Newark, cavalry saber given to Brigadier General Judson Fitzpatrick. 9 Sword made by Horster, Soligen given to Colonel H. F. Clarke.*

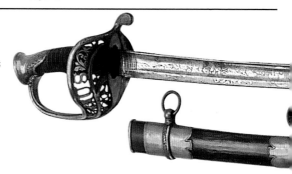

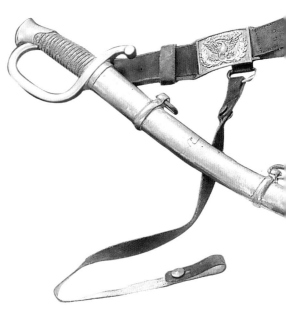

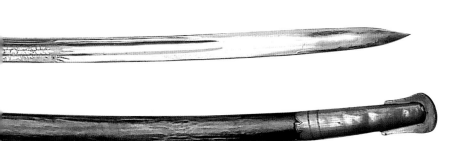

Above: Union Model 1850
Staff and Field Officer's sword.

Below: Union Model 1840
light artillery saber and
waist belt.

officers (brigadier generals and senior commanders) were all authorized to carry the Model 1860 Staff and Field Officers' Sword, which was a lighter, more decorated version of the Model 1850 weapon. This was the sword carried by the generals of both sides, and in most cases the weapons were personally owned by the officer, and were invariably of pre-war manufacture, purchased privately by the officer. It was similar to the Foot Officer's Sword, but it was usually more extensively decorated, and the letters "US" were cast into the hilt. The US Army's Model 1840 Non-Commissioned Officers' Sword was rarely used, but all sergeants and above were authorised to wear one. It had a straight $31\frac{1}{2}$ inch blade, and an all-brass hilt.

While the Confederates manufactured and issued their own Foot Officers' swords, they also produced Confederate versions of the Model 1940 Non-Commissioned Officers' Sword, even though it was clearly a waste of precious resources. Although these weapons were issued, the men who received them soon abandoned their swords in favor of

Below: *The white-bearded Brigadier General Edwin V. Sumner was the oldest active general officer of the War, commanding II Corps in the Peninsular campaign.*

more practical weapons, and from 1862 on it was rare to see a non-commissioned officer wearing a sword while on campaign. Like the Southern-manufactured cavalry swords, Confederate weapons tended to be cruder than the original weapons on which they were based, and usually lacked a stopper at the top of the blade (tang), and their grips were

simpler than the originals, being finished with untwisted brass wire.

Artillerymen were also authorized to carry swords, both in the pre-war army and in the two sides during the Civil War. Indeed this was officially the only form of personal weapon issued to artillerymen. The sword used by these gunners in field artillery units was the Model 1840 (M1840) light artillery saber, a weapon with a pronounced curve to its blade. The blade itself was 32 inches long and $1\frac{1}{2}$ inches wide at the hilt, with a single-barred brass guard which ended in a Phrygian helmet pommel. The weapon was carried in an all-iron scabbard. Some 20,757 swords of this type were purchased by the US Army during the war, although the weapon itself proved unpopular with the gunners who received it. It was found to be too light to parry a slash from a cavalry saber, while the weapon itself was clumsily balanced, and difficult to wield during a fight. It became increasingly common for gunners in both the Union and the Confederate army to acquire copies of the Model 1860 light cavalry saber instead of the artillery sword, as it was considered to be a far more practical weapon.

Instead of the Model 1840 saber, artillerymen serving in heavy artillery regiments were issued with the Model 1832 (M1832) foot artillery sword. These were the gunners who manned the large guns used in coastal fortifications, or operated the mortars and siege guns used by the Army of the Potomac.

The foot artillery sword was a direct copy of a French weapon, which was originally based on the gladius carried by Roman legionaries. While this example of the classicist revival may have looked impressive on the parade ground, the sword itself was practically useless as a weapon. Its

blade was only 19 inches long, while it was just under $1\frac{1}{2}$ inches wide at the hilt, giving it an unusual squat appearance compared to other contemporary military swords. It had an all-brass hilt with a molded brass grip, sculpted to resemble eagle feathers. The guard was a simple straight crossbar, while the pommel was formed into the image of an eagle surmounting a shield. The scabbard associated with this strange weapon was leather, with brass fittings.

Some 2,152 of these swords were purchased by the Army, but they were only used on ceremonial occasions. It can be argued that the production of this sword was a singular waste of money and resources, but surprisingly the Confederates produced their own slightly simpler version of this impractical weapon, even though their own resources were in short supply! Both of these two types of artillery swords were designed to serve as personal weapons in the event that the enemy would try to overrun an artillery

Below: *Union Model 1840 medical officer's sword.*

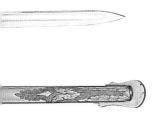

Above: *Union Model* 1840 *regulation foot officer's sword.*

battery. Once gunners gained some experience of warfare they abandoned their swords in favor of revolvers, which were better suited to the purpose, and which were less liable to get in the way of the gunners as they worked. Similarly sheathed knives were also carried extensively by gunners in both the Confederate and Union armies, and were far more useful than any ceremonial sword.

Musicians were issued with their own slightly shorter version of the NCO's sword. Known as the Model 1840 (M1840) Musician's sword, these weapons lacked the counterguards of the NCO's sword, and were never designed to be practical weapons, but just like the weapons issued to officers, they denoted the special status afforded to the wearer.

Finally, the US Navy issued its ships with cutlasses, for use during boarding actions. While this might appear anachronistic in the days of ironclads and powerful shell-firing naval ordnance, this type of action was one which the navy continually expected to fight. During the long years of blockade when the Union Navy placed blockading squadrons off the Confederate ports, boarding parties were routinely sent to inspect or seize other ships, and the sailors who formed these boarding parties were armed with both revolvers and cutlasses.

Even during the Battle of Hampton Roads when the Confederate ironclad CSS *Virginia* was fighting the Union ironclad USS *Monitor*, the commander of the *Virginia* planned to attempt to ram and board the enemy vessel. The boarding party would wedge the turret so it was unable to rotate, and would then throw grenades down the funnel and ventilator shafts in order to force the enemy ship to surrender. Although the boarding attempt was never made, it

Below: *Model 1850 Union foot officer's sword with German silver scabbard.*

demonstrates how important boarding actions were to naval commanders during this period. The Model 1860 (M1860) Naval Cutlass was a weapon with a slightly curved blade and a 25-inch blade. Its grip was formed from a wide piece of brass, which gave the hand a high degree of protection, while the grip was wood covered in leather, and surmounted by a flat brass pommel. It was carried in a leather scabbard,

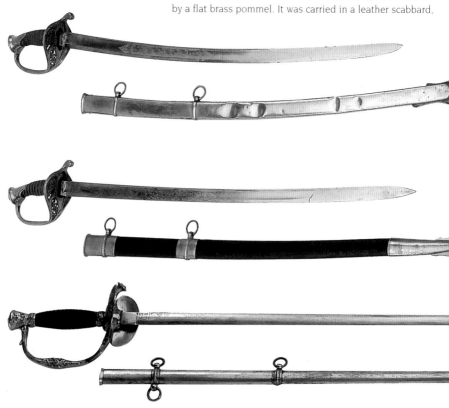

Right: *The pose is betrayed by the eyes. On his lap is a Model 1855 pistol carbine. Later, he may have been one of the many to send their saber home as a memento, adjudging it to be no more than a nuisance in the field.*

Left: *Union Model 1850 foot officer's sword, with brass-mounted leather scabbard.*

Below: *Union Model 1860 staff and field officer's sword.*

designed to be attached directly to the sailor's belt. This practical and utilitarian weapon was introduced to replace the more elaborate Model 1841 (M1841) Naval Cutlass. This earlier weapon had an all-brass hilt, the grip formed in the style of eagle feathers, and its straight blade was 21 inches long, making the weapon look completely different from the traditional design for a naval cutlass.

Naval officers carried the Model 1852 (M1852) Naval

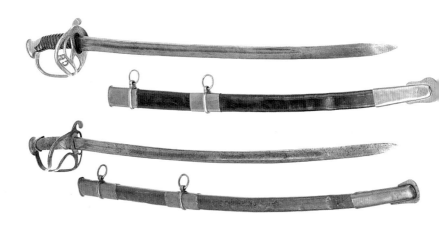

Above: *Confederate Leech and Rigdon staff and field officer's sword variant (top); and Confederate engineer officer's sword made by Boyle, Gamble and Co (bottom).*

Below: *Saber of Brigadier General Archibald Gracie, Jr., killed at Petersburg, 1864; made by Louis Haiman and Brother.*

Officers' sword, which was similar to the weapon carried by Foot Officers, although earlier weapons were also retained in limited numbers. The only real difference between the Navy and Army versions of the weapon is that the naval sword had a white fishskin grip, and it was engraved with nautical motifs. Officers were also issued with their own version of the M1860 Naval Cutlass, with the letters "US" or "USN" cut into the guard, but otherwise the weapon was the same as that carried by the sailors. Sailors did not go into action armed solely with cutlasses. Rifled muskets were issued to ships for use by designated marksmen. The standard weapon used was the Model 1861 (M1861) Whitney

Naval Rifle, a 0.69-inch caliber weapon . In addition some 6,000 Sharps & Hankins breech-loading carbines were purchased by the US Navy, while most sailors taking part in boarding actions or forming landing parties were issued with revolvers in addition to their cutlasses. The most common weapon used was the Colt Navy revolver, although other weapons were also used extensively.

In the Confederate Navy, cutlasses were also issued to ratings, the design based on the Model 1861 weapon, and of a comparable quality. The Confederate Naval Officers' sword was British-made, but was based on the M1852 officers' sword issued in the pre-war US Navy. However, a distinctive gold-plated dolphin's head design was used to decorate the backstrap and pommel, a design more commonly found on European rather than American swords during this period. Additional nautical decoration was cast into the guard, or used as decoration on the scabbard fittings, and like its Union counterpart the blade itself was often engraved with nautical motifs.

In addition a number of Southern sword makers produced their own weapons under contract with the Confederate Navy, or had their weapons purchased privately by naval officers. The scabbards used by the officers in both the Union and Confederate navies were made from leather, with brass fittings.

Bayonets and Knives

The bayonet was widely issued to infantry units during the war. Introduced at a time when the musket was a cumbersome weapon with a low rate of fire, the bayonet offered some degree of protection against cavalry. By the time of the Napoleonic Wars it was felt that a spirited

Above: *Short sword and wooden scabbard of the Confederate Foot artillery; more or less the weapon of a Roman legionary.*

bayonet attack could turn the tide of battle, and the weapon had become an essential part of the infantrymens' armament.

A feature of the Civil War was the way in which the fighting developed along modern lines, and it was not simply a repeat of earlier conflicts in Europe, despite the training and expectation of many of the officers and volunteers who rallied to the flag. In Europe, the bayonet was considered an essential military tool. However, in the decade before the Civil War began the rifled musket had entered widespread service, and was both more accurate and more reliable than the smoothbore weapons that had preceded it. This meant that firepower became more effective, and consequently the importance of the bayonet lessened.

Almost every type or model of military longarm had its own design of bayonet associated with it. Given the variety of longarms found on the Civil War battlefield, a similar variety of bayonets was to be expected. The typical bayonet of the war was a socket type, where a tubular sleeve fitted over the end of the musket barrel, and was locked into place by securing it around a lug on the tip of the musket barrel. The bayonet ran parallel to the musket barrel when it was

Below: *Union socket bayonet and scabbard; socket bayonet, scabbard and frog (bottom).*

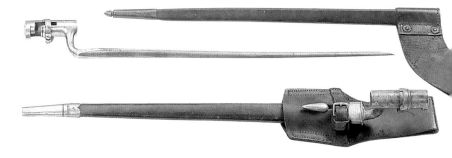

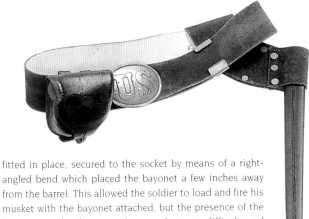

fitted in place, secured to the socket by means of a right-angled bend which placed the bayonet a few inches away from the barrel. This allowed the soldier to load and fire his musket with the bayonet attached, but the presence of the bayonet made the operation much more difficult and cumbersome. The blade extended an average of 18 inches from the muzzle, which changed the center of balance of the weapon, making it harder to load, cock, and aim. Therefore the attachment of bayonets was considered a last resort, or was undertaken by an attacker who wanted his men to hold their fire until they reached the enemy line.

Most bayonets were steel, with blades of a triangular section, tapering to a sharp point, with deep grooves (fullers) running the length of the upper edge of the blade. In theory these were designed to assist the soldier in extracting the bayonet once it had been used to stab an opponent. These "three-square socket bayonets" were most commonly associated with the Springfield muskets which made up the bulk of infantry long arms during the war, but a wide range of other bayonet designs were also encountered. These ranged from short blades the length of a hunting knife to larger weapons, which could be used as swords in their own right, complete with grips and guards. An example of

Above: *Union cap box, waist belt and bayonet scabbard.*

Opposite: *A bayonet and side knife pressed into cooking duties.*

the latter is the slightly curved sword bayonet provided for use with the British P1853 "Short Enfield" rifle, which combined the functions of a sword and bayonet into one. The sword bayonet of the Brunswick Rifle (a German design which was also used in the British Army) was even modeled on the gladius sword used by the legionaries of Ancient Rome, and therefore resembled the impractical weapon issued to heavy artillerymen pic tured on page 137.

The most common bayonet to see service during the war was the Model 1855 bayonet, produced by the Springfield Armory. It was designed to fit the Springfield Model 1855 rifled musket, but the same bayonet was also suitable for

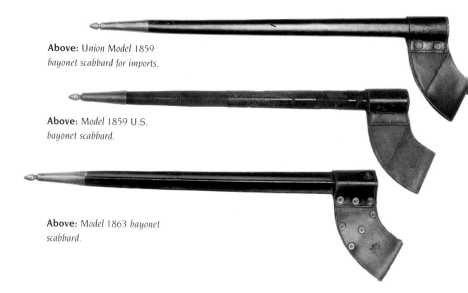

Above: *Union Model 1859 bayonet scabbard for imports.*

Above: *Model 1859 U.S. bayonet scabbard.*

Above: *Model 1863 bayonet scabbard.*

Right: A *bayonet that we can be sure was bloodstained.* Colonel E Elmer Ellsworth and his 11th New York Fire Zouaves were the first to take the Stars and Stripes back across the Potomac on May 24, 1861, following so many setbacks for the Union. Marching up the main street of Alexandria, the Colonel saw a secessionist flag flying defiantly from the Marshall House Hotel. Accompanied by Private Fancis Brownell he entered the hotel and tore down the flag. The proprietor, James T. Jackson, killed the Colonel with a shotgun. Brownell immediately emptied his musket into Jackson and finished him with his bayonet. Brownell poses with the bloodstained flag beneath his heel. Sixteen years later Brownell received the Medal of Honor for his action.

use with the more common Model 1861 rifled musket, and its successor the Model 1863. The Confederates produced their own version of this bayonet in the Richmond Armory, and like its Union counterpart the Confederate bayonet could fit both the M1855 and M1861 rifled muskets, whether produced in the north or the south.

A feature of most Confederate bayonets is that they were designed without grooves on the blade, which was considered an unnecessary addition to the original design. Another 0.69-inch caliber socket bayonet was widely used in association with older weapons such as the Model 1842 and even the Model 1816 smoothbore weapons, and the bayonets remained in use with these guns even after they were rifled, or converted to percussion fire, or both.

Short rifes were usually fitted with a sword bayonet, more because that was the way the guns were designed in Europe than due to any inherent tactical need by the soldiers using these weapons. The Model 1855 saber bayonet was designed for use with these shorter guns, and several variants were produced where the bayonet was adapted to fit a range of widely-issued weapons.

Compared to the straightforward design of a socket bayonet, a sword bayonet was a far more complex weapon, involving brass or steel fittings which were considered superfluous on regular bayonets.

Most of these bayonets proved too heavy and too awkward to use with any effect, at least as a bayonet rather than as a sword, and they fell from favor. Manufacture of saber bayonets had ceased by 1864 in the Confederacy due to a lack of materials, and while production continued in the

Above: *Union Model 1855 rifleman's waist belt and saber bayonet.*

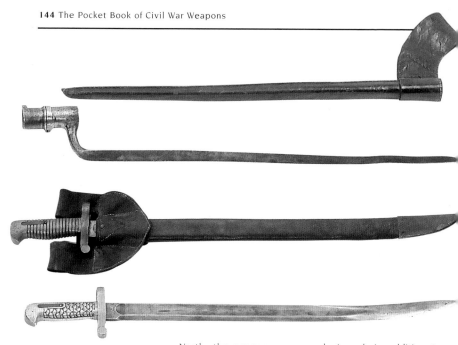

Above: *Confederate Raleigh Bayonet Factory socket bayonet and scabbard (top); Georgia Armory saber bayonet in scabbard (middle); Fayetteville saber bayonet (bottom).*

North, the weapons were rarely issued. In addition to American-made bayonets, thousands of P1853 socket bayonets were issued for use with the Enflield rifled musket, while the Pattern 1854 Austrian bayonet also saw widespread use with the Austrian weapon, which was widely imported by both sides during the war. These bayonets were specifically designed for their own type of weapon, and could not be exchanged with any other bayonets.or be used with any other arm.

Almost all bayonets were carried in a specially constructed leather scabbard, usually fitted with iron or brass fittings and suspended from the soldier's belt, immediately behind his left hip.

Obviously the scabbards associated with saber bayonets

were more elaborate, and many bore a passing resemblance to the scabbards used for full-sized swords.

The bayonet was not a popular weapon during the war, largely because of its restrictive effect on the use of muskets. Soldiers used them in a variety of non-regulation ways, such as woodcutting tools, digging implements, as tent pegs or even as candle holders! Most soldiers never expected to use their bayonets in anger, but the weapon still retained an important psychological value. Less than half of 1% of wounds or fatalities inflicted during the war were caused by the bayonet, but it was still important as a means of inspiring soldiers to launch themselves into the attack, or as weapons to be used in an emergency during hand-to-hand fighting.

A more useful weapon in these circumstances was the knife, an essential and often non-regulation part of the soldier's assemblage during the war. In the first months of the war both sides issued their troops with large knives, often with cumbersome "D-shaped" guards, the product of state armories resulting from experience gained either in the Mexican-American War or in fighting against the Native Americans.

More commonly soldiers carried their own knives, usually hunting knives or smaller sheath knives worn suspended from the belt. While some home-grown knives had fearsome blades over a foot long, most soldiers relied on a simpler, smaller tool. After all, for most of the time it served as a useful piece of equipment in the encampment, and it was only on the rarest of occasions that the soldiers expected they would have to use them in battle.

Similarly, knives were issued to all sailors in both the Union and the Confederate Navies, while boarding axes and

Above: *Confederate side knife made by Boyle, Gamble and Co., Richmond.*

even boarding pikes were carried on board ships for use in a boarding action. Their issue recalled the age of fighting sail, when fierce boarding actions were common.

Right: *Confederate naval arms and accoutrements. The British Pattern 1859 cutlass-type bayonet in its scabbard was designed for the British Wilson breechloading rifle below it. The short-barrelled pistol is for warning flares. The naval cutlass in the center has a canvas waist belt. The cutlass on the right was made by Thomas, Griswold and Co.*

Following pages: *Union naval arms and accoutrements. The pike was intended for use in boarding of Confederate warships. The muzzle-loading percussion pistol is US Navy Model 1842. The Bowie-type bayonet on the left was manufactured by Dahlgren. The cutlass in the center is the officer's Model 1860 design; below it is the Model 1841 design.*

During the Civil War in the very few instances where such engagements were fought, the sailors tended to rely on revolvers or cutlasses to do the job.

ARTILLERY

Artillery was always the least glamorous branch of the army, and the most professional. While infantry volunteers could take part in glorious charges, or cavalrymen ride against the enemy saber in hand, the gunners had a dirty, arduous, and dangerous job. However, artillery was a battle-winning weapon, and ordnance played a crucial part in the war, from firing the first shots against Fort Sumter in April 1861, to the last shot, (apparently) a final salute at Appomattox from a Confederate Virginia battery in April 1865.

Right: *Confederate artillery batteries in Charleston open fire on Fort Sumter on April 12, 1861. The war had begun.*

Artillery placed a crucial role in the Civil War. Given the raw nature of both armies when the conflict began, the support of artillery batteries in both attack and defense was of paramount importance, the presence of the guns bolstering the morale of the inexperienced troops. This

importance continued as the war progressed, as greater emphasis was placed on the use of entrenched positions, and warfare often became a struggle for control of fixed points. While the full benefits of artillery on the battlefield was sometimes limited by the dense woodlands in which many battles were fought, the guns could dominate clear lanes of fire, and even at point-blank range they could shred an attacker using canister fire.

During this period artillery was classified in several ways; by the weight of the projectile it fired, by the size and construction of the bore of its barrel, and even by its ability to be transported from one position to another. The most important classification was between field artillery and heavy artillery. Field artillery, was by far the most common type. Effectively it included all the artillery that could be used on the battlefield, and which could be moved with relative ease. Field guns were relatively light and mobile and were the type most commonly used to support the battle lines of the army during an engagement. The category of heavy artillery encompassed all the guns which were too large or cumbersome to fit into the former category. These pieces were further sub-divided into siege artillery and coastal artillery. Siege weapons were considered still mobile enough to keep pace with an army as it advanced, and could be deployed to pound enemy fortifications into submission. On occasion they could also be deployed in a defensive role, as happened during the Siege of Petersburg. Coastal artillery was primarily used in coastal fortifications to protect ports from attack from the sea. These guns were massive pieces which could only be moved with great difficulty, and therefore for all practical purposes were considered static pieces of ordnance.

Opposite: *Thirty-three hours of bombardment saw 3,341 cannon balls and shells fired at Fort Sumter. By war's end, the damage woold be far worse and the fort would be reduced to rubble. This photograph was taken in 1863.*

Above: *12-pounder Napoleons, Battery DeGolyer, Vicksburg; Capt. Samuel DeGolyer died here directing fire on the Confederate Great Redoubt.*

All types of artillery, whether field guns or heavy guns were further categorized by the trajectory of the projectiles fired by the pieces. Most artillery pieces of the period were classified as guns, which meant they had a flat or relatively flat trajectory, and were fired directly at the target. These direct fire weapons included most types of field artillery, and almost all coastal pieces. Howitzers resembled guns, but they generally had shorter and lighter barrels. While they could use direct fire, howitzers were also capable of firing in an arc, so the shot could pass over an obstacle directly in front of it to hit a target beyond. The longer the range to the target, the more pronounced was the arc of the howitzer's trajectory. This indirect fire capability was particularly useful when firing at fortifications. The final category was the mortar, which had a very short barrel and usually a far larger bore than most guns or howitzers. Although its range was limited it was a pure indirect fire weapon. A mortar projectile would climb steeply, then plummet to the ground, proscribing a high arc in the process. Like the howitzer, this was an ideal weapon to have during a siege, but it was of extremely limited use on the battlefield. For this reason almost all mortars were used solely as siege artillery.

Artillery pieces were also classified according to whether

Left: *11-inch mortar. "Indirect fire," firing at an unseen target on the battlefield, was almost unheard of at the time of the War, so mortars like this were reserved for sieges.*

a barrel was smoothbored or had been rifled. While most guns early in the war were smoothbore pieces, the proportion of rifled guns increased significantly during the war, particularly in the Union army. The advantage of a rifled piece was that, like a rifled musket, it had a far longer range than a smoothbore piece, and could be fired with considerably more accuracy.

Although the introduction of rifling cannot be dated with any precision, it is clear that rifled firearms had emerged by the end of the 16th century. It was first introduced as a way to reduce the pervasive problem of barrel fouling in early smoothbore weapons. Gasper Zollner of Vienna at first attempted to counter this problem by cutting two straight grooves into the walls of the barrel, these being intended to capture most of the fouling. However, gunsmiths had observed the archer's technique of achieving greater distance and accuracy by angling the flights to spin the arrow. By cutting twisting grooves down the barrel, then hammering the ball down tightly so that it engaged the grooves, the ball was spun upon firing and produced great improvements in performance. The depth and number of grooves steadily increased, rifled weapons of the 1800s generally having between three and twelve grooves. By the end of the 19th century, almost all weapons except shotguns were rifled, and even the shortest handgun barrel had rifling.

Rifling works on a simple principle. In flight, any object will try to present its heaviest face first and is also subject to the interference of wind, temperature, humidity, air pressure, and other factors. A bullet fired from an unrifled barrel, therefore, is prone to twisting erratically in flight, forcing it to deviate from its intended flight path. A rifled barrel, however, spins the bullet (or artillery shot and shell)

Opposite: *An early breech-loading cannon. The cannon in the gin appears to be a conversion. Although all artillery would become breech-loading in time, very few cannon were not muzzle-loading in the War.*

around its central axis, canceling the effect of weight shift and also making it more resistant to environmental interference. The consequence is a far more accurate round, which will fly further and hold its velocity for longer.

Finally, artillery was divided into breech-loading or muzzle-loading guns. Breech-load artillery was a recent invention, although the method had been used then abandoned during the Middle Ages. From the 16th century onwards, with the exception of small anti-personnel guns

Left: Union British Whitworth
breech-loading rifle, breech
mechanism removed. The
advantage of breechloading—
rapid fire and the ability to put
the projectile directly into the
rifling grooves —was sometimes
offset by a quick failure rate.

Below: Unidentified
Confederate breech-loader. The
Columbus Iron Works in
Georgia even built their own
experimental breech-loading
cannon, revealing the expertise
of the company's employees:
but they only produced one.

and a few experimental pieces, all artillery was loaded by
ramming the charge and shot down the muzzle. During the
Civil War almost all artillery pieces were muzzle-loading,
although a handful of breech-loading guns made an
appearance on both sides. These were extremely rare, and
although breech-loading artillery would come to dominate
ordnance design in the years to come, during the Civil War
almost every piece of artillery was muzzle-loaded.

Guns could be manufactured from either bronze or iron,
bronze being more commonly found in smoothbore field
artillery pieces, while most rifled guns were cast from iron. A
few novel guns were also constructed from wrought-iron
using specialist techniques, but for the most part these
experimental guns were limited to coastal artillery pieces
and to naval guns. While bronze guns were relatively easy to
produce, the metal was unsuitable for the construction of
rifled guns, as the bronze was softer than iron, so guns

Right: Union gun crew with 20-lb Parrott gun. Usually, depending on the cannon, there were seven men in a crew. Gunner number two put the "cartridge" of ball amd powder in the muzzle. Gunner number one shoved the cartridge down the tube with the rammer. Meanwhile gunner number three kept his thumb over the vent hole at the breech; then with cartridge in place, he jabbed a wire through the vent to expose the black powder. Number four placed a primer in the hole. On command the lanyard attached to the primer was jerked to ignite primer and cartridge. Number one extinguished any embers with a soaked sponge rammed down the barrel. Gunner number five handed the next cartridge to number two. Gunners six and seven manned the ammunition chest and supplied number five; if the projectiles were shells, they cut the fuses to suit the anticipated flight time to target.

tended to deteriorate more quickly and the rifling would become worn away too quickly. Civil War field artillery lacked any kind of recoil mechanism and therefore the piece would jump when it was fired. This meant that after every shot most guns had to be aimed at the target again. Simple recoil mechanisms were incorporated into the design for the carriages of some siege or naval guns, largely because the process of aiming the gun again after every shot would have been prohibitively slow, and the recoil might damage the ship or fortification in which the gun was housed.

Artillerymen used a wide variety of ammunition types, depending on the task they were asked to perform. The traditional solid shot cast-iron cannonball was still used, as it had been on land and sea for centuries before. A more streamlined bullet-shaped solid projectile was designed for use by rifled guns, although where grooves in the projectile would connect with the rifling in a similar manner to the way a minié ball worked when it was fired from a rifled musket. Both smoothbore guns and rifled guns could also fire shell as well as solid shot. Shells were hollow metal projectiles

Left: *Probably the first picture taken of the Union Army in combat. The photograph is by the celebrated Mathew Brady, who organized a corps of photographers to follow the troops in the field. The long exposure time and the cannons' roar caused camera shake.*

Previous pages: *Field artillery projectiles. Left-hand page, clockwise from top left: Union 20 lb Parrott shell; 3-inch Absterdam solid bolt; 10 lb Parrott shell; 3-inch Hotchkiss canister; 10 lb Schenkl shell; 3-inch Hotchkiss solid bolt; 20 lb Schenkl shell; 8 lb solid shot; 12 lb solid shot. Right-hand page, clockwise from top left: Confederate 10 lb Parrott shell; 3-inch Mullane shell; 3-inch Reed shell; 10 lb Parrott shell; 3-inch Reed-Parrott shell; 3-inch Burton shell (minus sabot); 12 lb British Whitworth solid bolt; (above) 12 lb British Britten shell (minus sabot); 1-inch Williams solid bolt; 12 lb British Whitworth shell.*

Right: *Union horse-drawn Model 1841 six-pounder. This carriage was also used for both 2.9-inch and 3-inch Parrott rifles, the 3-inch Ordnance rifle, the 3.8-inch James rifle, and the twelve-pounder field howitzer.*

which were filled with an explosive charge. This was an ideal type of ammunition to use against large bodies of troops in the open, or against wooden structures.

Both shot and shell were used at all ranges, but at close range a gun crew would often switch over to some kind of case shot, designed for use against human targets. There were three main types of case shot, each being used either by certain gun types, or against certain types of targets. Shrapnel was essentially a form of shell which could be fired with great effect so that it exploded directly over the heads of a body of enemy troops. Fragments of shell would then rain down on the troops below.

Grapeshot was another anti-personnel round, and when fired it sprayed out a hail of miniature solid shot projectiles; perfect for ripping apart enemy infantry or cavalry at medium

range. Finally there was canister, fired at point-blank range. It sprayed an enemy with a hail of small musket-sized balls, and could cut great swathes in the ranks of an attacking infantry formation. Most guns were capable of firing all of the types of ammunition mentioned above, while howitzers were limited to just shot and shell. Mortars were limited to firing shell and shrapnel. The decision of which type of round to use depended on the type of target being fired at,

Above: *Roundshot stacked at the Washington Arsenal. Lincoln's fear of a Confederate attack on the Capital kept the city well-garrisoned and armed throughout the War, even when troops were sorely needed elsewhere.*

Below: *Shells from both sides destroyed the Henry family home at 1st Manassas. The occupier, the widow Mrs. Henry, was killed during the battle.*

and on the range. For instance an artillery piece might fire solid shot at an infantry regiment which was advancing towards it, then switch to shrapnel, then grapeshot; and finally it would use canister when the enemy were within a hundred yards or so of the gun.

Smoothbore Artillery

At the start of the war the most widely available piece of field artillery available to either side was the Model 1841 (M1841) bronze 6-pounder smoothbore. This gun had first seen service during the Mexican-American War, where it performed extremely well. It was light enough to be extremely mobile, yet it could fire quickly, and with good effect. Its maximum effective range was around 1,500 yards at 5° of elevation, and was designed to fire solid ball at ranges from 600 yards onward, with its maximum range given as 2,000 yards. Within 600 yards it would switch to canister. It was also able to fire shells against buildings or soft targets, making it a versatile and dependable weapon. When the war began it had already been superseded by the newer and heavier Model 1857 (M1857) bronze 12-pounder smoothbore, a weapon popularly known as the "Napoleon." However, only five of these new guns had entered service before the fighting began, so the 6-pounder gun was the only smoothbore field piece available until both sides could produce their own pieces. The US Army ordered some 1,127 "Napoleons" during the war, while the Confederacy manufactured another 481 of their own. In addition the Confederates were able to augment their artillery arsenal with guns captured from the enemy.

The US Army had used 12-pounders before, but during the Mexican-American War it was found that these pieces were too heavy to keep up with the army on the march. Consequently ordnance designers came up with the "Napoleon" based on the experiences gained during the war. Compared to earlier 12-pounders it was lighter, its bronze barrel weighing 1,220 pounds, and it had an effective range of approximately 2,000 yards at 5° of elevation, which gave it

Right: As the War progressed, in some theaters the lines became more defined, and there was time to create defenses like these Confederate earthworks outside Atlanta.

Opposite: *Guarding Union 3-inch Ordnance rifles at City Point, VA, in 1864. By then the superior industrial might of the North had made defeat unthinkable.*

Below: *This destroyed 12-pounder may have been a Mountain Howitzer Model 1841; not easy to identify.*

an edge in both range and weight of shot over the M1841 smoothbore. Its nickname came from the French Emperor Napoleon III. The French Emperor was an artillery enthusiast, and he introduced a gun of this type into French service just before the Crimean War (1854-56), and the gun performed well during the campaign. The design was duly copied and adapted by the US Army Ordnance Bureau.

Confederate copies of the "Napoleon" were similar to the original US Army design, although the Southerners produced a number of cast-iron versions of the "Napoleon," with the barrels reinforced at the breech to compensate for

Right: *Captain John Pelham, or "the Gallant Pelham' as he came to be known, was a courageous and skillful artilleryman. At the Battle of Fredericksburg his two guns were deployed on the Confederate right flank. His guns kept up such a rate of fire and moved so frequently that they held up the advance of an entire Union division, who thought they were opposed by several Confederate batteries. He was killed in a cavalry skirmish at Kelly's Ford, Virginia in March 1863.*

any potential flaws in their home-spun gun-casting foundries. They performed well enough in action, as did the more conventional Confederate-produced "Napoleons," whose bronze barrels weighed 1,320 pounds, the extra weight compensating for the less pure bronze used in the casting compared to the US Government-produced pieces. Another characteristic of Confederate brass "Napoleons" was that they lacked the pronounced muzzle swell found on Union guns. Ever short of raw materials, the Confederate designers had redesigned the gun to save metal where they could, and the metal saved was redistributed to provide additional protection around the breech of the piece.

Like the 6-pounder, the 12-pounder "Napoleon" was designed to fire solid shot or shell from a range of around 600 yards to its maximum effective range (2,000 yards for solid shot, and 1,500 yards for shell). The artillery manuals stated that 300 yards was the minimum effective range for both these types of projectile, but shell was primarily seen as a long-range projectile. Below 600 yards the "Napoleon" would fire one of the standard forms of case shot at the target, saving its canister fire for the final 200-300 yards.

Both the M1841 and the M1857 were crewed by seven men, and the gun was mounted on a wooden carriage, painted olive green, and fitted with an elevating screw which helped the gunner aim his piece with speed and precision. Each gun was provided with a limber and a horse team (usually of six horses in the Union army, and four in the Confederate service), which gave the pieces a great degree of mobility, and allowed them to keep up with the advance of the infantry in an attack. The crew rode into battle on the limber box, which doubled as an ammunition storage box containing powder and shot. In addition, each gun was

Following pages:
Smoothbore Model 1857 Napoleon. The weapon number and date of manufacture are around the muzzle. The view is from the Confederate defenses at Peachtree Creek, Atlanta, Georgia, looking back toward the city.

accompanied by an artillery caisson which carried extra ammunition as well as a spare carriage wheel, in case one was damaged while the gun was in action. Each battery was accompanied by its own traveling forge, and by a battery supply wagon. While both sides used other types of smoothbore guns during the Civil War, these two 6-pounder and 12-pounder pieces were far and away the most common types of artillery on the battlefield. While the 6-pounder formed the mainstay of the artillery arm of both sides during the first year of the war, most 6-pounder batteries were replaced by 12-pounder batteries as they became available. Redundant Union 6-pounders were either placed in reserve depots or re-issued to the US Navy, who used them as boat guns on small launches. Most 6-pounders in Confederate service were eventually melted down to provide bronze for the casting of more powerful 12-pounder "Napoleons." The new guns were a godsend for the Confederates, as the Union army was able to re-equip its batteries at a far faster rate than the Southerners.

In late 1862 General Robert E. Lee wrote to the Secretary of War to explain how his 6-pounder batteries were being outclassed by the enemy's 12-pounder "Napoleon" batteries, and he urged the government to speed up production. His plea clearly had an effect, as by the time of the Gettysburg campaign in the summer of 1863, most smoothbore guns in the Confederate Army of Northern Virginia were 12-pounder "Napoleons".

The Union Army had no need to melt down old guns, but could simply order what it needed. While the initial design and the first batch of pre-war guns were produced by US Government foundries, wartime production of the "Napoleon" was contracted out to five privately-owned

Opposite: *Fort Morgan, one of the three forts defending the stategically important Mobile Bay, Alabama. The pentagonal bastioned fort of brick on the extreme western end of Mobile Point had an earthen water battery housing seven heavy cannon at its base. A Union fleet under the command of Rear-Admiral David G. Farragut ran past the guns of the fort, forcing its way into Mobile Bay on August 21, 1864. After Farragut had defeated the Confederate flotilla in the bay the fort was isolated, and consequently it surrendered two days later.*

foundries. The army ordered 179 of these weapons from these five foundries in 1861, and production increased to 422 pieces in 1862, and a further 512 pieces in 1863, at which point production was stopped as the army found itself with a surplus of the weapons. A further 26 guns were ordered by individual states, the majority being requested by Massachusetts, who were supplied with 18 pieces for use by their own state troops. Obviously all other volunteer artillery batteries were incorporated directly into the US Army, and were supplied by them. Incidentally, Union artillery batteries consisted of six guns in three sections of two guns apiece, while Confederate batteries contained just four guns, in two sections of two guns each.

In addition to these smoothbore guns, the US Army also developed a series of field howitzers. These pieces tended to have shorter barrels than standard field guns, and came in a range of sizes, the most common being the 12-pounder, 24-pounder and the 32-pounder field howitzers. Although larger howitzers existed, they were classified as heavy artillery, and formed part of the siege artillery category. The Model 1841 (M1841) 12-pounder howitzer was the most commonly encountered artillery piece of this type, and its bronze barrel weighed just 788 pounds, compared to the 1,220 pounds of the 12-pounder "Napoleon" field gun. While the "Napoleon" had a barrel length of 72 inches (6 feet), the stubbier M1841 was just 53 inches long. It had a maximum range of 1,322 yards and an effective range of 1,072 yards at 5° of elevation (1,500 yards when firing spherical case shot). This made it a useful gun, capable of being dragged into firing positions which were impassable to heavier pieces of ordnance.

Even more remarkable was the Model 1841 (M1841) 12-pounder mountain howitzer, a gun designed to be broken down into sections (barrel, trail, and wheels) so it could be carried by pack mule. This small but powerful little gun was just under 33 inches long, and its barrel weighed just 220 pounds, although its range was roughly comparable with the larger 12-pounder howitzer. While Model 1844 (M1844) 24-pounder howitzers and model 1844 (M1844) 32-pounder

Right: A Confederate artilleryman's kepi. Red was the color for the artillery branch on both sides.

howitzers were officially classified as field artillery pieces, they rarely saw service, the majority of the howitzers operating in the field being 12-pounder pieces. However, small numbers of the larger guns did see service.

For example, while most Confederate howitzers were 12-pounder pieces, at least two Confederate batteries which participated in the Antietam campaign (1862) included two 24-pounder howitzers apiece. Effectively the 12-pounder M1841 howitzer was rendered obsolete by the arrival of the 12-pounder "Napoleon", which fulfilled all of its functions, and was a more powerful gun. After all, it was a smoothbore gun which could also fire shells, traditionally the exclusive preserve of the howitzer.

In most European armies, artillery batteries consisted of a mixture of both field guns and one or two howitzers. The arrival of the "Napoleon" removed the necessity for this kind of deployment, but the practice continued through much of the war, as both sides retained a number of howitzers in batteries which also included the new smoothbore guns. What kept howitzers in service throughout the war, at least in limited numbers, was their lightness and mobility. It could also elevate further than the "Napoleon", making it useful in certain situations, such as the attack on enemy-held heights, or when firing shell at extreme range. The Confederates made their own howitzers, both in brass and iron, but the pieces were considered inferior to their Union counterparts.

Rifled Guns

Like infantry longarms, rifled artillery pieces were simply guns with a series of spiral grooves cut on the inside of the barrel, designed to make contact with the projectile as it

Left: *Union patent havelock cap or "whipple hat" with battery insignia.*

was fired. The result was a weapon that was more accurate than its smoothbore counterpart. This improved accuracy was largely due to windage and spin. Windage was a measure of the difference between the size of the bore of the gun and the diameter of the projectile. Clearly the shot needed to be slightly smaller than the bore in order to load the piece, but the larger the gap around the projectile, the less efficient the effect of the explosion which propelled the shot out of the barrel. In rifled guns, the projectile locked itself into the rifling along the inside of the barrel, which reduced the windage to nothing. This meant that without the lessening of the velocity of the piece through windage, rifled guns could shoot their projectiles farther than smoothbore guns could. The other factor was also a feature of the rifling, imparting spin to the projectile and thus ensured that the shot flew in a straight line, at an almost flat trajectory, as explained earlier. The combination of high velocity and accuracy proved a deadly combination.

Right: *Various Confederate artillerymen's buttons. Millions of buttons were made during the War, primarily of die struck sheet brass. Huge numbers were imported from England.*

However, rifled guns did have their disadvantages. One was that they used a form of semi-fixed ammunition, where the cartridge containing the explosive propellant and the actual projectile were both loaded separately. With smoothbore guns, the two were usually together, much like the cartridge of a rifled musket. With rifled pieces the two were kept separate owing to the extra care it took to load the rifled projectile as there was far less windage. As a consequence it took far longer for a crew to load a rifled gun than a smoothbore piece, and therefore smoothbore guns had a greater rate of fire, which helped in part to make up for the lack of relative accuracy.

The US Army had two types of rifled field artillery in its arsenal when the war began, the 3-inch Ordnance rifle and the 10-pounder Parrott rifle. A former army officer, Robert Parker Parrott was the superintendent of the West Point Foundry in New York, and shortly before the war he developed a rifling system which he applied to a range of

R R
P re
A

rifled pieces of various calibers, ranging from the 10-pounder to an enormous 250-pounder rifle, designed for use in coastal fortifications. Several experimental versions of the weapon had been ordered by the Commonwealth of Virginia before the outbreak of the war, and these served as the pattern for Confederate versions of the gun. While Parrott himself admitted that his design was not perfect, his guns were available, and could be produced in significant numbers. The Model 1861 10-pounder Parrot had an iron barrel with virtually parallel sides, and a heavy reinforcing band strapped around the breech, which gave the barrel a distinctive shape. The same design was also used on all larger versions of the Parrott design. The barrel weighed 890 pounds, making it comparable in weight to a 6-pounder smoothbore, and considerably lighter than a 12-pounder "Napoleon". A more significant difference was the range. While a "Napoleon" had a maximum effective range of 1,500 to 2,000 yards, the 10-pounder Parrott was highly effective out to more than 2,000 yards, and had a maximum effective range of 3,000 yards at 5° of elevation. Its listed extreme range was no less than 5,000 yards, or almost three miles!

Parrott patented his rifled gun in 1861, and production began at his West Point Foundry immediately afterwards. His original 10-pounder (M1861) had a 2.9-inch bore, but in 1863 this was increased to 3 inches (M1863). The weapon proved extremely effective, and during the war the US Army acquired 587 M1861 Parrott rifles, making it the second most common rifled gun of the war. A further 58 copies of the gun were produced in Richmond's Tredegar Ironworks, while a further batch of less satisfactory copies were produced in Macon, Georgia. The Confederates also produced limited numbers of copies of the larger 20-pounder Parrott rifles, 45

Opposite: *Federal artillery officer's uniform coat with distinguishing red trim.*

in Richmond and an unknown quantity in Macon. The 20-pounder entered service in the Union army during late 1861, but it proved a less satisfactory field piece than the lighter 10-pounder. The M1861 20-pounder Parrott had a barrel weight of 1,750 pounds, making it twice as heavy as the smaller gun, and although its range was a little greater, the

Right: *The Union made no less than seven major drives against Richmond in the course of the War. By the winter of 1864-65 life for the citizens had settled into an awful routine of searching for food and fuel amid the rubble. This kind of damage—whether by artillery, fire, or deliberate Confederate destruction—brings nothing so much to mind as the bombed cities of World War II.*

additional benefits were not thought to be sufficiently worthwhile to replace the 10-pounder with the heavier weapon. It was only used in limited quantities. Although the 20-pounder Parrott was the largest true field piece of the war, a handful of 30-pounder Parrotts saw limited service in the field.

The Model 1861 (M1861) 3-inch Ordnance Rifle was one of the finest field artillery pieces of the war. Developed at the same time as the Parrott Rifle but designed along slightly different lines, the weapon was produced by the privately-owned Phoenix Iron Company of Phoenixville, Pennsylvania. The company employed a mass-production technique which meant that the weapon could be produced for just under $300, making it twice as cost-effective as the 10-pounder Parrott rifle, and slightly more expensive than a "Napoleon" smoothbore. Versions of the gun were also cast in limited numbers by the Singer-Nimick Company of Pittsburgh and Henry N. Hooper & Company of Boston. The barrel weighed just 800 pounds, and was shaped with a distinctive swell toward the breech, like an old-fashioned soda bottle. The 3-inch rifle had similar performance characteristics to the 10-pounder Parrott rifle, but it was considered to be a far more reliable weapon. During the war only one 3-inch rifle burst while it was being used, while accidents were more common with the Parrot weapon. The US Army purchased some 935 of the weapon, making it the most widely used rifled gun of the war. Robert E. Lee's artillery chief Edward P. Alexander referred to the weapons as "beautiful," and it was no wonder that when the Confederates captured examples of the weapon, they copied the design. The Tredegar Ironworks in Richmond and the Noble Brothers & Company foundry in Rome, Georgia, both produced approximately 150 copies of the weapon.

While most rifled artillery pieces was muzzle loading, a handful of breech-loading weapons saw limited service during the war. These were the products of two British manufacturers, Armstrong and Whitworth. These pieces were regarded as the most accurate weapons on the

Opposite: *Rodman on the inner lines of the Confederate fortifications at Petersburg, 1865. By this stage of the war the Union army had an overwhelming superiority in this type of heavy gun, and the Confederate gunners found themselves outclassed and outgunned.*

battlefield, and were much prized, both in the army and at sea, but their cost was prohibitive, and only a handful ever saw action in Confederate service. The Whitworth 6-pounder (2.17-inch caliber) rifled gun and the 12-pounder (2.75-inch) rifle were superb weapons, produced by the Whitworth Ordnance Company of Manchester in England. They were extremely accurate, and with a maximum range of 10,000

Below: *15-inch Dahlgren, Washington DC, August 1864. 34 of these monsters were built by the Fort Pitt Foundry between 1862 and 1864. This mighty gun would never be fired in anger in the War.*

yards they could outshoot any other gun on the battlefield. Fortunately for the Union, only a few of these weapons made it through the Union blockade. The Armstrong 12-pounder was a similar weapon, and could fire a projectile out to 2,100 yards with perfect accuracy, at double the range with near perfect precision. The Confederate army of Northern Virginia deployed a battery of four Whitworth breech-loading rifled guns during the Antietam campaign, and the weapons

Right: *A captured Confederate eight-inch Brooke gun slung on a Confederate sling cart, James River. When the attempt to cast five 6.4-inch double-banded Brooke rifles failed, they were bored-up to this 8-inch smoothbore.*

proved incredibly effective. Though all breech-loaders had a tendency to sieze.

Finally the US Army adapted standard 12-pounder "Napoleons" by rifling their barrels as an experiment, but these proved less than satisfactory, and the practice never became widespread. However the Confederates captured a large quantity of semi-obsolete smoothbore guns in US Arsenals at the start of the war, and many of these pieces were adapted into rifled weapons. General Charles T. James had perfected the process of converting smoothbores into rifled pieces before the war, the Confederates employed this technique to produce limited numbers of "James Rifles". The problem with these was that as most barrels were originally cast from bronze, the rifling was prone to wear at an alarming rate, and so the guns were of limited use; more a stop-gap measure than anything else.

Siege and Coastal Artillery

The same methods of categorizing field artillery by caliber, weight of projectile, and method of fire, also applied to the larger guns used in siege trains or in coastal fortifications, although of course the gun sizes were substantially larger. These guns were virtually immobile, and once set up in their firing position they could not be moved without considerable effort. Clearly the rate of fire of these weapons was much slower than with field artillery, pieces. Some of the largest siege or coastal artillery pieces could fire no more than 12 rounds per hour, while even the lightest coastal guns were limited to a maximum rate of fire of under 20 rounds during the same period.

Large smoothbore guns were becoming obsolete as the war began, through the development of new forms of heavy rifled artillery. However, large quantities of these smoothbore weapons were deployed in seacoast fortifications, including the Model 1839 18-pounder, the Model 1819 24-pounder, the Model 1829 32-pounder, and the Model 1841 42-pounder smoothbore guns. While these guns might have been of limited use as individual weapons, most coastal fortifications deployed their guns in large batteries and in several tiers of brick or stone casemate batteries. This meant that the combined weight of fire of whole batteries of these pieces was considered sufficient to drive off most attacking warships. The development of the ironclad meant that these guns became obsolete overnight, but they were eminently suitable for the defense of fortifications against wooden vessels. Many of these older guns on the open upper level of forts or in siege positions were mounted on barbette carriages, where they could swivel around a central or frontal pivot.

Opposite: 50,000 *lb* (25 *tons*) 15-*inch Rodman gun at Fort Monroe, VA. Rodmans were cast using the Rodman process of internally cooling a hollow core (a system referred to as "wet chill").

Other coastal artillery pieces were mounted on more conventional carriages in casemates. This meant they fired through a small aperture, so their field of fire was limited. These weapons were trained using a slide mechanism which resembled a small railroad track set into the floor of the casemate.

A far more impressive type of gun was the Columbiad smoothbore, which first saw service in 1844. The Model 1844 8-inch Columbiad weighed an impressive 9,240 pounds, but it could fire an eight-inch shell at a range of just under 5,000 yards. This, and its counterpart the 10-inch M1844 Columbiad, became the principal heavy gun used in coastal

Below: *Ten-pounder Parrott rifles and shells inside Fort Putnam, Charleston, South Carolina; three grooves with a right-hand twist.*

fortifications, and it was also adapted for use by the US Navy, and with less effect as a mobile siege weapon. 15-inch (M1861) and 20-inch (M1864) Rodman Columbiads were also produced, but these pieces were almost prohibitively cumbersome; the 20-inch weapon weighed 115,200 pound (57 tons), although it fired a one ton projectile 8,000 yards. However, these 15-inch and 20-inch Columbiads were guns

Above: *In 1861 Charleston dignitaries had visited Fort Sumter to survey the armaments captured. Four years later their own city lay in ruins.*

deployed in coastal fortifications that were destined to never fire a shot in anger. It was only the coastal fortifications in the Southern states which ever came under attack, where the principal armament was limited to 8-inch and 10-inch Columbiads, and to the smaller more obsolete smoothbore heavy guns.

The introduction of rifled guns into both siege trains and coastal fortifications revolutionized heavy artillery. The 30-pounder M1861 Parrott rifle was the smallest siege gun available during the war, but it was .a highly effective weapon, and could be transported without too much difficulty. The effectiveness of rifled guns of this type was

Below: *This photograph is believed to be of Fort Fisher, North Carolina. It was protected by no less than 50 cannon, among them fifteen heavy Columbiad smoothbores and an eight-inch Armstrong rifle. After a disastrous Federal amphibious assault, a second attack, following a huge naval bombardment, was successful on January 15, 1865.*

Left: Castle Pinckney in Charleston Harbor was used successively in the War as a fort, prison and artillery position. Federal POWs taken after 1st Manassas were lucky if they were sent here, with sufficient food and good shelter. After these prisoners were removed, the fort was returned to defensive service when the range and power of the Federal bombardment increased. Mortars and four Columbiads were mounted on the barbette tier of the fort. Castle Pinckney's position allowed it to fire on ships moving toward Charleston in the main Harbor Channel; though it never did. The Columbiads are still there today, too heavy for the relic hunters.

Above: *Confederate mortar battery at Pensacola, Florida; photographed at the beginning of the War, the men wear all kinds of uniforms.*

Left: *The Dutch Gap on the James River, VA, being fortified with ten-inch mortars.*

demonstrated during the attack on Fort Pulaski which guarded Savannah in Georgia.

Parrott rifles were able to fire on the fortification while remaining beyond the range of the smoothbore pieces deployed inside the fort. As a result Fort Pulaski was battered into submission in little more than a day. This served as a highly effective demonstration of the impotence of smoothbore guns compared to rifle pieces, but as the former were already deployed in significant numbers, the Confederacy to could do little to improve its lot.

In addition to conventional guns, large howitzers were also used in both siege trains and in coastal fortifications during the war. The Model 1844 24-pounder howitzer and the Model 1841 8-inch howitzer saw service in both fortifications and as siege weapons, while they were also deployed to protect static field fortifications such as the entrenchments built to protect Washington DC. The larger Model 1841 10-inch howitzer was solely deployed in coastal fortifications. The advantage of the 8-inch howitzer as a defensive weapon was that it could fire canister rounds containing 48 iron balls, making it a very effective weapon for the point-blank defense of a fortified position.

Right: *Improvised mobile artillery at Petersburg, 1864. The 13-inch coastal mortar mounted on the railroad flat car is the famous "Dictator."*

Both sides made a limited use of mortars. Model 1841 (M1841) 8-inch mortars and Model 1841 (M1841) 10-inch mortars siege mortars or seacoast mortars plus the monster Model 1841 (M1841) 13-inch seacoast mortar were all used to considerable effect. A new version of all these weapons was produced in 1861, but the M1861 mortars were only produced in limited numbers during the war. A large number of siege mortars were used in the siege of Yorktown in 1862, although the Confederates withdrew before the bombardment began. The trouble was, it just took a lot of time and effort to dig the emplacements for these weapons, and to deploy heavy siege artillery so that the weapons could be used to maximum effect. When more time was available, as at the Siege of Petersburg (1864-65), mortars and heavy siege guns were used to better effect. One feature of the siege of Petersburg was the use of the huge Model 1861 13-inch seacoast mortar known as "the Dictator." The 17,120-pound (8.5-ton) mortar was mounted on a specially strengthened railway platform car so that it could be moved on the Petersburg & City Railroad within the Union siege lines in front of the Confederate-held city. This allowed the mortar to reach a range of points on the Confederate defensive line or to fire its shells within the Petersburg perimeter. When the mortar fired the railroad car would recoil 12 feet down the track. Weapons of this type had range of up to 4,200 yards, and their fire had an extremely demoralizing effect on the enemy.

The Confederates produced their own copies of the Model 1841 10-inch and 13-inch mortars, and they also seized a large quantity of these weapons at the start of the war. The majority of which were deployed in defensive positions around the Confederate coasts.

Below and opposite: *The Vandenburgh volley gun. When General Origen Vandenburgh of the New York State Militia could not find a buyer in Europe, he sold to the Confederate Army.*

The Confederates also imported a small number of heavy guns from Britain. These pieces were some of the most modern guns of the age. Four 70-pounder (5-inch) Whitworth rifled guns were captured on board a Confederate blockade-runner and then used by the Union army during the Siege of Charleston, South Carolina. However, a number of Blakely rifled guns managed to reach the Confederacy,

and were used to help defend fortified positions. The most famous of these was "The Widow Blakely," a 7.5-inch rifled gun which had been converted from a British 42-pounder smoothbore piece by Blakely, then shipped over. It formed part of the defensive works of Vicksburg during the summer of 1863. In addition the Confederates acquired two 8-inch Armstrong rifles and one of these was used in the defense of

Opposite: *The Gatling's chief virtue was its rugged simplicity; inconsistency in ammunition was one of the main reasons for any stoppages.*

Fort Fisher near Wilmington, North Carolina. This piece weighed 15,737 pounds (7.9 tons) but it was probably the most effective piece of heavy artillery in use during the war.

Rapid Fire Weapons

While machine guns are not technically regarded as being artillery pieces, they were viewed as such during this period.

Dr. Richard J. Gatling of North Carolina was the inventor of the first effective machine gun when his design was first patented in 1862. Production began in a Cincinnati Foundry in 1863. A six-barrel weapon, the gun worked by rotating the barrels around a central spindle using a hand-operated crank. Paper cartridges were pre-loaded into metal sleeves containing a percussion cap, and these were fed into a hopper designed to drop the cartridges one by one into the each of the breeches when the barrel arrived in its firing position. However, the mechanism proved troublesome and prone to jamming. 12 Gatling guns were manufactured during 1862 but they were rejected by the US Army Ordnance Department and were purchased privately by General Benjamin Butler, who used them during the Petersburg campaign of 1864. In that year Gatling modified his original design to incorporate copper rimfire cartridges, which proved to be a significant improvement, and the weapon went into widespread production immediately after the war. The rest is history, as the gun became phenomenally successful, until superseded by the Maxim Gun.

The Confederates produced their own machine gun in 1862, a year before Gatling, but the weapons were less effective than the Gatling design. These weapons were the brainchild of Captain Williams of Kentucky, who mounted a heavy barrel on a one-horse carriage based on the design for the M1841 mountain howitzer. Paper cartridges were loaded manually into a compartment in the breech, and percussion caps were also fitted before firing. Once the weapon was set up it could be fired by means of a hand-operated crank, and in theory it was capable of sustaining a firing rate of 60 rounds per minute. However, it took a long time to reload between volleys, and while reliable, it was considered little more than a novelty on the battlefields; although the Confederate Ordnance Department ordered 42 of the

weapons, and they first saw service during the defense of Richmond in 1862.

In late 1861 the US Army purchased 10 experimental Agar machine guns, nicknamed the "Coffee Mill" by Union troops. With these weapons a special steel cartridge was fed into a large hopper mounted above the breech of the weapon, and a hand-operated crank was used to fire the gun by dropping the cartridges through a sifter and into the breech. Each turn of the crank performed two firing cycles. The Agar was officially adopted as the "Union Repeating Gun" in 1863, and 63 of the weapons entered service with the army the following year. However it proved unreliable and the weapons were not used in the field. In theory the Agar was

Right: *A cartridge entering the Gatling breech during loading. Just a few years after its production a well trained team of men could achieve a rate of fire of about 1,000 rpm.*

capable of firing 120 rounds a minute, but its tendency to jam made it unlikely it could ever fire more than a few rounds at a time.

The Billingshurst-Requia "covered bridge gun" incorporated an unusual arrangement of 25 rifled musket barrels arrayed in a line. A thin metal strip holding steel cartridges was fed into the breech of the line, and all barrels were discharged at the same time. The device could be loaded quickly and easily, and it was reasonably efficient. However, the device only saw limited service in the Union Army as a defensive weapon in field fortifications.

Finally, the Vandenburgh volley gun was a short, stubby weapon with multiple barrels encased in a single cylindrical casing. Several versions of this experimental gun were produced with 85, 91, and even 451 barrels. A pre-loaded plate of copper cartridges was slotted into the breech, (in an early version each barrel had to be individually loaded) then locked in place using a large screw press, which made an airtight seal with the firing chamber. Groups of barrels could be fired, or alternatively the whole lot could be discharged simultaneously with a single percussion cap in the center of the breech, a spectacular event which produced a virtually prohibitive recoil. While considered impressive, the weapon was considered impractical, and was never adopted by the US Army. The example shown on page 203 was captured by Union Cavalry near Salisbury, North Carolina, in April 1865, and is now exhibited in the museum at the United States Military Academy, West Point.

During the Civil War machine guns were in their infancy, but the experimental weapons which emerged during the conflict would help pave the way for the horribly practical machine guns that would appear in the following decades.

Right: *Memorial at the Tupelo National Battlefield site, Mississippi. Major General Andrew J. Smith was tasked with ensuring that the Confederate cavalry of Major General Nathan B. Forrest did not attack Sherman's railroad supply line in middle Tennessee, hampering the campaign against Atlanta. Smith advanced south on July 5, 1864 from LaGrange, Tennessee. Forrest's commander, Lt. Gen. Stephen D. Lee, ordered an attack on Smith's force of some 14,000 men for the morning of July 14, 1864. But the attacks were uncoordinated and easily beaten back, the Confederate artillery ineffectual. Confederate losses were double those of the Union, at 1,300.*

NAVAL WEAPONS

❖

While there were no epic naval battles with terrible losses as there was on land, both the Union blockade of the southern coastline and the activities of the river gunboats had a significant effect on the course of the War. Both sides built up their naval strengths during the war, and armed their warships with some of the most powerful guns of the era. The Confederates used new technology to counter the Union superiority in ships and men by deploying mines, submarines, and torpedo boats against the blockading fleet.

Right: *The USS Miami's pivot gun crew goes through a training exercise with the 11-inch Dahlgren.*

Below: *Deck of the* USS Monitor *on the James River in July 1862. Note the shell dents.*

Naval ships were essentially weapons systems in their own right, and their design and employment was crucial to their effectiveness in an era when naval technology was

changing rapidly. The most spectacular innovation during this period was the development of the ironclad, an armored steam-powered warship which was proof against virtually any guns then carried on board conventional wooden-hulled warships. The duel between the CSS *Virginia* (formerly the USS *Merrimac*) and the USS *Monitor* off Hampton Roads, Virginia, on March 9, 1862 was the first fight between two ironclad warships, and it ushered in a whole new phase of naval evolution. The engagement was a stalemate, as the armament of both the Confederate and the Union ironclad was insufficiently powerful to penetrate the armor-plating protecting the enemy ship.

Far more impressive was the previous day's sortie into Hampton Roads by the *Virginia*, when the Confederate ironclad was opposed by nothing but wooden-hulled Union warships. During the short engagement she sank the USS *Cumberland* and the USS *Congress* without sustaining any significant damage herself. At that moment all existing wooden-hulled warships had become obsolete. For the rest of the war the Confederates stuck to the design they developed for the *Virginia*; a low freeboard vessel stripped of everything above the waterline apart from a large iron-plated casemate, which resembled an upturned cast-iron bath with gunports cut into its sides. Over a dozen casemate ironclads entered Confederate service during the war, including the CSS *Tennessee* which saw action in Mobile Bay (1864), the CSS *Albemarle* which defended the coastal waterways of North Carolina, and the CSS *Arkansas*, which was built in the remote Yazoo River, and ran through the Union blockade outside Vicksburg in 1863. For their part Union designers came up with several ideas for ironclads, but the success of the USS *Monitor* at Hampton Roads meant

Below: *Captain James Alden's*
USS Brooklyn *(far right)*
leads the Union line into
Mobile Bay in one of the Civil
War's key naval battles. When
Alden stopped under heavy fire
to find and clear mines,
Admiral David Farragut,
aboard the USS Hartford, *is*
reported to have shouted,
"Damn the torpedoes! four bells
[or full speed ahead]."

that the design was adopted as the basis for all future Union ironclads. Designed by the Swedish-born inventor John Ericsson, the vessel was smaller than its Confederate counterpart, and its low freeboard meant that the hull of the vessel was largely underwater. The most visible feature was a single armor-clad revolving turret, designed to house two powerful 11-inch Dahlgren smoothbore guns. Later monitor designs were created with larger hulls, or with more than one turret, but the same basic design which according to one observer resembled "a cheese box on a raft" was used by the US Navy throughout the war.

The *Monitor* and the *Virginia* were not the first ironclads in

the world. That honor went to the French, who launched the revolutionary ironclad *Gloire* in 1859. She resembled a conventional steam-powered warship, except that her hull was protected by iron plating, creating a casemate which

Below: *Officers of the* USS Monitor. *Side armor was 30 inches, five layers of one-inch iron over 25 inches of oak.*

was impervious to enemy fire. The British responded with their own series of ironclad warships, the first of which was the graceful and powerful HMS *Warrior,* which entered service in 1860. Unlike American ironclads the British and the French opted for larger vessels with a higher freeboard, which meant they could be used on the open seas. The drawback of the monitor design was demonstrated when the original *Monitor* foundered in rough seas of Cape Hatteras in December 1862.

The introduction of the steam engine during the early 19th century meant that by the time the Civil War began, all first-line warships in the US Navy were powered by steam, either using a screw propulsion system or more unusually a sidewheel paddle system. A handful of sailing ships were retained, but their effectiveness was limited. When the war began the US Navy consisted of 90 ships, of which 21 were considered unfit for service, and the bulk of the remainder were either deployed overseas, or were undergoing extensive repairs. In order to have enough ships to institute a blockade of the Confederate coastline the US Government hired or purchased hundreds of civilian steamers and converted them into warships, while dozens more vessels were ordered from Northern shipyards. This meant that the bulk of the Union fleet continued to consist of wooden steam-powered ships, often powered by vulnerable sidewheel paddles. While less than ideal in action against Confederate warships, many of these newly acquired ships were fast, and well-suited to chasing blockade runners. The Confederate began the war in an even worse position, as it had no navy whatsoever. The Confederate Secretary of the Navy Stephen Mallory realised that he was unable to match the shipbuilding capacity of the Union, nor could he purchase more than a handful of civilian steamers and press them into service. Instead he chose to rely on new technology to help offset the Union's numerical advantage.

This meant that the meager resources of the Confederate Navy were used in the production of new and revolutionary weapons systems; ironclads, commerce raiders and torpedoes. The ironclad program has already been discussed, although it is worth noting that it was an extremely ambitious undertaking, and the Confederates used considerable ingenuity to overcome the industrial and technological limitations of Southern shipyards and

Below: *This Confederate submarine was recovered after the war from the Mississippi River near New Orleans. It was originally fitted with a small conning tower, and was armed with a spar torpedo.*

foundries. A crucial factor in the success of the ironclad program was the selection of the armament for the ships, and the Confederates were fortunate to have ordnance experts who were able to develop naval guns which were extremely effective.

Commerce raiding was a state-run version of the privateering which for centuries had been an important

element in naval warfare. The Confederate Navy adapted or commissioned a series of high-seas commerce raiders which could scour the oceans in search of Union merchant shipping. This program was highly effective, tying up large numbers of ships and men in the effort to hunt these raiders down. Vessels such as the CSS *Florida* and the CSS *Alabama* were custom-built for the task, and were armed with the latest British ordnance which made them the equivalent of the US Navy's cruisers sent to track them down.

Torpedoes (the equivalent of modern mines) were a different matter. Unlike modern torpedoes these were defensive weapons, the forerunners of the underwater mine, although in some instances torpedoes could also be used on land. The sophistication of these weapons increased as the war progressed, and several Union warships were sunk after hitting them. They were also transformed into offensive weapons, first by attaching them to long poles or spars which projected from the front of steam launches, to be rammed into the side of an enemy ship, so detonating the torpedo. More sophisticated torpedo boats followed, and the both sides also experimented with the use of submarines, whose offensive weapon was the torpedo. The most famous torpedo attack of the war was that conducted by the Confederate submarine CSS H.L. *Hunley* against the Union wooden steam-powered warship USS *Housatonic* off Charleston Harbor (1864). Although the attack was a complete success and the *Housatonic* was sunk, the Confederate submarine never returned to her base. Her wreck was recently discovered and her remains were raised.

Another unique feature of naval warfare during the Civil War was the use of shallow-draft warships on the Mississippi River and her tributaries. Both sides build

Below: *Engraving from Harper's Weekly in early 1862 of Commodore Andrew H. Foote's gunboat flotilla on the Mississippi. In the foreground is the flagship USS Benton. Originally she was a catamaran-hulled riverboat. The two hulls were planked over to make one hull 72 feet wide and 202 feet long. Leading the attack on Fort Henry on February 6, 1862, she was hit 32 times but continued to close to within 600 yards and help force surrender.*

substantial fleets of river gunboats, while the Union also constructed a series of shallow-draft, lightly-armored casemate ironclads, designed solely for use in the waters of the Mississippi basin. The first baptism of fire of these craft came during the attacks on Fort Henry and Fort Donelson in February 1862, when it was discovered that their armor was barely adequate. However, they continued to be used to fight their way down the Mississippi River to Vicksburg, and demonstrated their superiority over conventional wooden-hulled gunboats in the process. This "Brown Water Navy" which the US Navy employed on the Mississippi soon grew into a formidable force, and its presence was felt far into the Confederate heartland, as the vessels could operate in all but the shallowest of creeks or rivers. Another innovation used during this Mississippi campaign was the deployment

Above: USS Baron de Kalb, Mound City, *and* Cincinnati *at Cairo, Illinois. These were the first ironclads, known as the City class, of which there were seven vessels built by civil engineer James B. Eads and designed by naval constructor S. M. Pook.*

Following pages: USS Tuscumbia *tied up in the western rivers, 1863. Inboard of her are two mortar rafts.*

of mortar rafts. Large quantities of 10-inch and 13-inch mortars were mounted onto wooden rafts, and then towed into position by steamboats. This meant that the Union could bring its siege weapons to bear wherever it wanted on the river and its tributaries, a crucial element in ensuring Union victory during the campaign.

One strange tactical doctrine of the time was the notion that the ship itself could be used as a weapon by ramming the enemy. Many warships of both sides built warships with specially reinforced bows, specifically for the purpose of sinking the enemy by ramming. The CSS *Virginia* used her ram to sink the USS *Cumberland* off Hampton Roads in 1862, but the attack proved less than successful, and the Confederate ironclad damaged herself slightly during the attack. Most Confederate ironclads were designed to be used as rams, but their lack of speed and propulsive power meant they were unsuited to the task. The tactic proved more successful on the Mississippi River where the Confederates built several steam-powered wooden rams, and even managed to sink a Union ironclad using the tactic. Despite this, the ram was seen as something of a novelty weapon, although it continued to b considered a legitimate option in naval combat. With the odd exceptions of the ram and the offensively-used torpedo, naval combat was dominated by gunnery, and both sides developed their own distinctive approaches to the problem of equipping their ships and using them in action.

Shell Guns
Civil warships, whether ocean-going, coast or inland water vessels, or riverine craft, were all capable of deploying guns which were in general terms larger and heavier than the

pieces used on land. They were floating weapon platforms, and their armament could to some extent be altered according to the role the vessel was expected to perform. At the outbreak of the Civil War the US Navy was fairly well advanced in gunnery compared to its European rivals, largely through the introduction of shell-firing guns in the years leading up to the war.

These were the invention of naval ordnance expert John Dahlgren who introduced a series of extremely effective shell guns during the 1850s. A shell gun was a weapon which fired explosive projectiles. Not only did these cause more damage than solid shot, they also added to the danger of fire in an age were warships were almost exclusively built from wood.

The US Navy experimented with shell guns during the 1840s, but these weapons were not entirely successful, and it was not until Dahlgren introduced his 9-inch smoothbore shell-gun in 1850 that the situation was rectified. The 9-inch gun M1850 fired a 72-pound shell and weighed 1,000 pounds. It soda-bottle shape was the result of Dahlgren's design where the breach was heavily reinforced. The gun continued to be used extensively throughout the Civil War.

His next gun was an 11-inch smoothbore shell gun, which first appeared in 1851. It weighed 1,700 pounds and fired a 136-pound shell or a 165-pound solid shot. This was the gun used in the ironclad USS *Monitor*, although it was also used extensively used on Union steam-powered wooden warships. During her duel with the *Virginia* off Hampton Roads in 1862 the *Monitor's* shot failed to penetrate the armor of the Confederate ironclad, so Dahlgren increased the powder charges for his guns, which greatly increased the hitting power of the weapons.

Opposite: *Pennsylvanian John Adolph Bernard Dahlgren, who designed the heavy iron deck cannon, the Dahlgren gun, while at the Ordnance Department of the Washington Navy Yard, the most important naval gun of the War. He was appointed Rear Admiral in February 1863 with command of the South Atlantic Blockading Squadron. Not a talented (or popular) leader at sea, after the war he returned to his metier to command the Washington Navy Yard.*

Following pages: *Gunners from USS Hunchback load a 12-pounder field-mounted Dahlgren howitzer.*

By the time the war broke out he had also introduced a 10-inch smoothbore shell gun (designated the M1853), capable of being used on a small pivot carriage on smaller ships than ones capable of carrying their heavier 11-inch gun. In 1854 the Navy contracted to produce 156 9-inch guns and 14 10-inch guns for use in a new class of steam-powered wooden frigates, making those vessels some of the most powerful warships afloat before the development of the ironclad.

For the most part carriages for these guns were based on the French Marsilly design, and were little different from those used for conventional naval guns, apart from the fact that the Marsilly carriages had no rear truck-wheels, in an attempt to limit the recoil of the guns. As the gun and carriage of a 9-inch Dahlgren weighed over five tons, aiming these weapons at the target was a problem, and so weapons which were not mounted on wooden carriages in large gundecks were mounted on pivoting carriages, which had a

Left: USS Sangamon was *a 1,335-ton Passaic Class monitor built at Chester, Pennsylvania. During most of 1863 she served in the James River. In early 1864 she was transferred to the blockade off Charleston, South Carolina, but returned to the James later in the year. In March and April 1865, she took part in operations to clear mines from the river.*

Opposite: *The steam frigate, or sloop, USS Pensacola off Alexandria, Virginia, in 1861. The Pensacola was a Hartford Class frigate, one of five. She mounted 20 guns and later in the War had a pivot eight-inch rifle converted from a Dahlgren smoothbore. Their impressive firepower and relatively moderate draft made the Hartford Class ships a natural choice for actions against coastal fortifications. For service against Forts Jackson and St. Philip and the taking of New Orleans, April 24-25, 1862, the boy Thomas Flood and Captain of the Foretop James McLeod of the Pensacola would each receive the Medal of Honor.*

far greater arc of fire. They resembled the carriages used in coastal fortifications, in that the gun and carriage moved along a metal rail set into the deck, or else pivoted around a fixed point, usually located against the hull of the ship.

Other warships employed an even more ambitious system whereby the gun could be fired on either the port or starboard side of the vessel, and the whole gun and carriage moved from one side of the ship to the other along a series of rails. This meant that a warship could carry fewer guns than usual, but could carry heavier ones than before. During the war Dahlgren produced three more guns, the 13-inch, the 15-inch and the 20-inch smoothbore shell guns, all designed in response to the development of Confederate iron-clads. The 15-inch gun, weighing 42,000 pounds (21 tons) entered service in 1862, and fired a 440-pound solid shot or a 330-pound shell. It was useful that Dahlgren guns could fire both types of ammunition, as while the shell proved highly effective against wooden vessels or shore positions, only solid shot could batter its way through the armor plating of an enemy ironclad. Its effectiveness was demonstrated when the USS *Weehawken* armed with two guns of this type forced the submission of the Confederate ironclad *Atlanta* near Savannah in 1864. The drawback with these heavy armor-smashing guns is that they took a long time to reload, with a maximum rate of fire of no more than 12 shots per hour. In general the 11-inch and 13-inch Dahlgren smoothbores were probably the most useful weapons in the naval arsenal, as they could be operated faster than the larger guns, but still had a powerful punch. His largest gun was a 20-inch smoothbore shell gun weighing 100,000 pounds (50 tons). Although these were bought by the Navy in 1864, they never saw service before

Right: USS Pittsburgh *was a Cairo Class ironclad river gunboat. She was damaged during the bombardment of Fort Donelson, Tennessee. After repairs she continued in action on the Mississippi. In April 1863 she was one of the vessels that ran past the Confederate batteries at Vicksburg and attacked fortifications at Grand Gulf.*

Opposite: *The USS Morse was a converted civilian steamer, which took part in, among other engagements, the capture of Fort Powhatan on the James River, July 14, 1863. She was also ordered up the York River in support of the infamous Dahlgren Raid on Richmond in March 1864. The failed attempt to free Federal prisoners revealed papers on the dead body of Colonel Ulric Dahlgren that seemed to exhort his men to assassinate President Davis. Whether the papers were a forgery is still debated. The reaction in the South was outrage and plans to blow up the White House.*

the end of the war, despite being the most powerful naval guns then in existence. It has been estimated that 1,185 9-inch and 465 11-inch Dahlgren guns were produced during the war for use by the US Navy, while a further 113 15-inch and 11 13-inch guns also entered service. These guns proved so effective that many of them remained in service for decades after the end of the war.

Rifled Naval Guns

The principle of rifling was obvious to naval gun designers but was not until 1860 when Robert P. Parrott developed his first weapon that an effective rifled gun entered service with US Navy. His first guns, the 10-pounder, 20-pounder and 30-pounder Parrot Rifles have already been described, and both of the larger weapons saw service with the Navy. The US Navy also commissioned its own version of the 30-pounder Parrott, which was a little lighter than the siege gun version of the gun, but which had a greater range, 4,874 yards at an elevation of 15°. In 1861 the 100-pounder Parrott entered service, a gun capable of firing a 6.4-inch projectile over five

Right: *USS Red Rover on the western rivers with an ice barge tied up to her port side. She was a a 625-ton side-wheel river steamer captured at Island Number Ten in 1862. She was used for the rest of the War as hospital ship for the Mississippi Squadron.*

Right: *A largely imaginary impression of the gundeck of the Confederate ironclad* CSS Virginia *(ex. USS Merrimac), as pictured by a French illustrator. The guns illustrated in this engraving are 110-pounder Armstrong breech-loading rifles. These guns were never carried on board the* Virginia. *Instead, she was armed with two 7-inch rifles, two 6.4-inch rifles, and six 9-inch smoothbores. A British Ordnance Select Committee sat in judgement of the new Armstrong guns in 1865: "The many-groove system of rifling with its lead-coated projectiles and complicated breech-loading arrangements is far inferior for the general purpose of war to the muzzle-loading systems and has the disadvantage of being more expensive, both in original cost and ammunition." The return to muzzle-loaders was a retrograde step that would give Germany a head start in the ensuing arms race.*

miles with extreme accuracy. The next Parrott was the 150-pounder Parrott rifle, a weapon which the US Army in their wisdom classified as a 200-pounder gun. It was comparable in weight to an 11-inch Dahlgren smoothbore piece, and could be fitted in a similar broadside mount or carriage as

the shell-fire gun. Of course it had a far greater range and velocity than its counterpart, and it was used in a series of both river ironclads and wooden gunboats. It was also fitted as a second gun inside the turret of some monitors, so that the ironclad carried a mixture of rifled and smoothbore

pieces. It fired a 152-pound shell or a 200-pound solid shot for just 4,290 yards at 13.5° of elevation, or a little under three miles, but its projectile weight more than made up for its lack of range compared to a 100-pounder Parrott.

For the most part Parrott rifles proved to be useful to the Navy and over 700 guns of various calibers were purchased by them during the war. However, when several 100-pounder and 150-pounder guns burst during the attack on Fort Fisher in 1864 and early 1865, the guns were temporarily withdrawn from service. It was later discovered that the build-up of residue in the barrel had caused the series of accidents, but by this time the reputation of the guns had been tarnished. John Dahlgren also produced rifled guns; 30-pounder, 50-pounder, 80-pounder, and 150-pounder rifles being produced during the war. These proved less successful than his smoothbore weapons, and several bursts during use made the Navy wary of issuing them in any number. In addition rifled guns were also developed by General Charles T. James as a means of re-using obsolete 42-pounder smoothbores which had been discarded by the army. These pieces were reworked so that they could fire an 81-pound solid shot or 64-pound shell. They were widely used in river gunboats during the early years of the war.

One of the main problems with rifled guns was that most naval engagements of the war were fought at close range, so the rifled guns used on warships were not used to their full potential. In general terms, they proved less successful than smoothbore pieces in naval service, although the Confederates developed their own type of rifled guns which proved to be highly efficient, and the Confederate Navy continued to favor these home-built Confederate pieces throughout the war.

Opposite: *Nine-inch Dahlgren shell gun aboard the* USS Hartford. *Eighteen thousand men of African descent served in the* US *Navy, 15 percent of the total enlisted force. Eight won the Medal of Honor.*

Confederate Naval Ordnance

The Confederate Navy proved to be more successful in providing its ships with reliable ordnance than it was in building reliable ships. The capture of the Gosport Naval Yard in April 1861 meant the Confederates managed to seize 1,200 heavy guns which supplied the Navy and the Army (who operated coastal fortifications) with most of their immediate needs. The haul included 9-inch Dahlgren guns, plus over a thousand 32-pounder smoothbore pieces, many

Above and left: *The blockade-runner* CSS Teaser *was captured by* USS Maratanza *on the James River on July 4, 1862. she was carrying detailed schematics of the new ironclad,* Virginia II, *which was nearing completion.*

Right: Sketch plan of the gun deck of ironclad CSS Louisiana, dated April 24, 1862; the day (or rather, the night) when David G. Farragut's fleet slipped past the formidable Forts Jackson and St. Philip and their 126 guns to force the surrender of New Orleans. During the preceding six-day bombardment of the forts—which had been largely ineffectual—the incomplete Louisiana had remained moored up, but turned her guns on targets of opportunity.

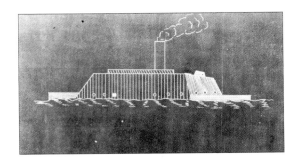

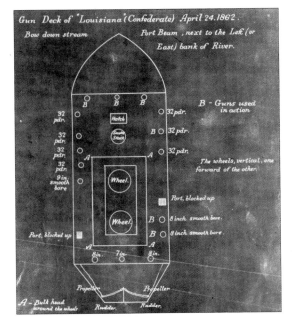

of which were later converted into rifled guns to increase their effectiveness.

During late 1861 the Confederates began converting the burned-out hull of the USS *Merrimac* into the ironclad CSS *Virginia*. The ordnance expert Lieutenant John M. Brooke was approached to design guns for the new craft, and the result was the first of a series of rifled naval guns which would become the mainstay of Confederate naval ordnance throughout the war. The *Virginia* was armed with ten guns; six 9-inch Dahlgren smoothbore shell guns, two 7-inch Brooke

Below: *One-hundred-pounder Parrott rifle on board the* USS Pawnee, *nine-inch Dahlgrens in the background. That does not look like a raw recruit. Both sides found it hard to find naval manpower. Initially, even experienced sailors were tempted to transfer to the Army by regimental bounties.*

Below: *Twelve-pounder howitzer "boat gun," aboard a Union Passaic Class monitor.*

rifles, and two 6.4-inch Brooke rifles. During the engagement against the USS *Monitor* the *Virginia* failed to penetrate the armor of the enemy ship, but this was largely due to her carrying shell rather than solid shot. Her commander had not expected to meet the *Monitor* that morning, and had

planned to engage the wooden ships of the Union fleet. The 6.4-inch and the 7-inch Brooke rifles were both extremely powerful and reliable guns, weighing 10,700 (5.4 tons) and 14,800 pounds (7.4 tons) respectively. While the Confederates never undertook systematic tests of the effectiveness of these guns, their performance in action demonstrated that they had the edge over Parrott rifles of a comparable size (100-pounder and 150-pounder Parrott rifles). The 7-inch Brooke rifle also had an effective range of 7,900 yards, which was significantly greater than either of the two Union guns.

These two types of Brooke rifle were used extensively by the Confederate Navy, and many ironclads, including the CSS *Atlanta* and the CSS *Tennessee* were armed exclusively with these two guns. In these circumstances it was usual to find the smaller pieces mounted on Marsilly carriages as broadside pieces, while the 7-inch Brooke rifles were mounted on pivot mounts, and deployed in the bow and stern of the armored casemate. In addition to these two weapons Brooke also designed a less successful 8-inch rifled gun, and an 11-inch rifle was designed for use in coastal fortifications.

Finally he produced a small quantity of a light 4.62-inch rifled gun for use on Confederate gunboats, plus a series of 8-inch, 10-inch, and 11-inch smoothbore shell guns which were modeled on the Dahlgren design. While Brooke rifles were powerful and had a great hitting power, it was argued that they were not as effective as smoothbore guns when used against wooden warships. Therefore several Confederate ironclads were armed with the smoothbores.

Confederate warships purchased abroad were often armed with foreign-manufactured weapons, including the

Following pages:

Confederate naval officers' uniforms and equipment. Such objects are extremely rare. This is hardly surprising, when the Confederate Navy probably mustered less than 5,000 men during the War, in comparison with the Union's 133,000. The three dolphin head naval swords (bottom) are among the most sought-after objects from all theaters of the War.

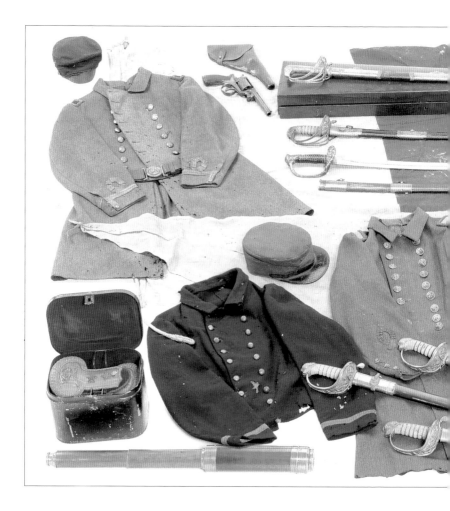

British Armstrong, Blakely, and Whitworth rifled guns and smoothbores. Of these the powerful 7-inch Blakely was carried on the CSS *Alabama* and on the CSS *Florida*, while 7-inch Blakely pieces were also mounted as single bow guns in the Confederate ironclads *Huntsville* and *Tuscaloosa*.

Above: *Acting Master Eben M. Stoddard (left) and Chief Engineer William H. Cushman of the* USS Kearsarge, *with 11-inch Dahlgren pivot gun.*

Torpedoes

Those "infernal machines", or torpedoes, are what we call mines today. During the Civil War they were found to be extremely effective as a means of protecting Confederate harbors and rivers. Commodore Matthew Fontaine Maury is best remembered for his oceanographic work but he was also the founder of mine warfare, responsible for the development of a series of torpedoes which were widely employed from the James River to the Mississippi River. Most early torpedoes were simple watertight containers, usually metal and shaped like a small barrel. These were filled with black powder, and then given some means of detonation. The simplest form of this was a length of fuse, lit shortly before the weapon was thrown into the sea. More commonly the torpedo would be fitted with a contact detonation device, which was usually a crude affair involving a percussion ignition system similar to that used on a standard firearm of the period.

In some cases the torpedo could be linked by a waterproofed electrical wire to the shore, allowing the device to be detonated on command. More sophisticated contact torpedoes relied on a chemical reaction when a glass container was broken, while others used purpose-built copper percussion devices similar to the contact devices used on the mines of the First and Second World Wars. As the war progressed the use of mines became increasingly widespread both in the Southern harbors and on the Mississippi River, and the devices used to detonate them became increasingly sophisticated. The most dramatic successes were achieved against enemy warships operating in confined waters, such as when the USS *Cairo* was sunk after hitting a mine on the Yazoo River, or the USS *Tecumseh*

Right: *Confederate "David" torpedo boat at Charleston, South Carolina, abandoned following the city's capture. Armed with a spar torpedo, in October 1863 a David vessel commanded by Lieutenant W. T. Glassell successfully attacked the Union warship USS New Ironsides off Charleston, damaging but not sinking it.*

Following pages: USS Galena *on the James River, June 1862. Not, strictly speaking, a casemate ironclad, but rather a gun boat clad in iron, she was actually quite poorly armored in comparison with* New Ironsides *and* Monitor*. The* Galena *was intended as an alternative design to the* Monitor*. The 180-foot vessel carried four nine-inch Dahlgrens and two 100-pounder rifles. On May 15, 1862 she tested Richmond defenses steaming up the James River and was severely damaged by the batteries at Drewry's bluff. The Union fleet was forced to withdraw.*

sank after striking a mine at the entrance to Mobile Bay. Of the several mine types used, the keg type was the most common; a small metal cylinder with pointed ends which could be moored just below the surface of the water, and detonated on contact. During the war Confederate torpedoes were responsible for the sinking of seven ironclads and 27 wooden gunboats, while another 14 Union warships were damaged by the devices. As well as their physical impact, these weapons also had a profound psychological effect on Union sailors, as they never knew when they were going to hit one of the devices.

In addition to using mines as a defensive weapon both sides also used them offensively, although it was the Confederates who made the greatest effort to sink enemy ships using torpedo-equipped vessels. The first torpedo boats were simply small launches fitted with spar torpedoes; torpedoes mounted on the end of a very long pole. Later, purpose-built torpedo boats were used, such as the David Class produced near Charleston, which were used with some effect during the defense of the city. A Union launch armed with a spar torpedo managed to sink the ironclad CSS *Albemarle* in 1864 while the Confederate was at anchor.

The Confederates employed torpedoes on submarines, making several less than successful sorties before achieving success against the USS *Housatonic* off Charleston. In the years that followed the navies of the world would develop the idea of the torpedo boat, while the mine and the torpedo would become separate types of weapon, although they still shared the same deadly purpose. Like many forms of warfare which was in its infancy during the Civil War, mine warfare would come of age during the decades which followed.

INDEX

Page references in **bold** refer to picture captions.